Life is on your side.

Acknowledgments

My heartfelt thanks go to Greg Yolen for his superb editing, designing and sense of humour, Leslie Kenton, for being the best 'Professional' I know, Frances Kennett, Hugh Synge and Maria Scaman who helped me become a writer, Paul, Lee and Dareen at Access Repro who always managed to get the job done yesterday and make it fun. There are many more. Thank you all.

To my son Greg
who made this book possible

Touchstone Publications
P. O. Box 57
Haslemere, Surrey GU27 2RW

First published in Great Britain in 1997
Copyright © Julia Hastings 1994
ISBN 09 52 0282 63

The Author asserts the moral right to be identified as the author of this work.The examples of mental picturing techniques and case histories in this book are completely general in nature and do not reflect personal disclosures from clients. The intent of this author is to offer helpful information of a general nature, not to dispense medical advice nor prescribe the use of any technique as a form of treatment for medical or psychiatric problems without the cooperation of your doctor or therapist. In the event that you use any of the information in this book for yourself, the author and publisher assumes no responsibility for your actions.

Cover by Greg Yolen
Book design and typesetting by
Touchstone Publications
Graphic reproduction by Access Reprographics
Printed by Guernsey Press

YOU'RE GREAT!

3 Steps To Self-Confidence

by Julia Hastings

Touchstone Publications

Born in California, Julia Hastings is a psychologist who specialises in coaching the technique of mental picturing. She works with many multinational companies, appears on television and radio gives talks and leads regular seminars. For more information write to:

P.O. Box 57, Haslemere, Surrey
GU27 2RW, England
EMail Address
106562.410@compuserve.com

CONTENTS

Self-confidence will make you irresistible

Chapter One

This Is It!

Have you ever noticed how self-confident people radiate an aura of strength and security? How they radiate a power of their own? These people are few and far between, but you can be one of them. There is a secret to feeling like this and that is to live your life in a way that is so motivating and mouth-watering to you that what other people think won't matter any more.

Feeling like this is called passion, or enthusiasm, which comes from the Greek word *en theos* which means to be at one with the Divine. Whether you call it passion or enthusiasm, with it your life has meaning, without it your life doesn't. When your life lacks meaning you feel cheated and left out. But you haven't been cheated by life, you've just left yourself out of it. You can dive back into life any time you want. It's waiting for you. To wholeheartedly live your life you need self-confidence.

The Secret Is Belief

The secret of self-confidence is to believe in yourself —

to have an unshakeable belief in yourself and your worth. It's easy to believe in yourself when life is going your way. It's easy to believe in yourself when your health is good, you have good relationships and plenty of money, but this is not always the case. You can lose your job, your partner, your health or your money. When you need it most your self-confidence deserts you. If you don't know how to get it back, you can end up never trusting yourself again.

The purpose of this book is to show you how to build up your self-confidence, so that even if things go wrong, you'll know who you are, where you're going, and how you're going there. This book will give you the tools to develop an *unshakeable* self-confidence that can never be taken away.

Happiness Is Your First Step

There are 3 steps to self-confidence. The first step is to have clear goals and to make sure happiness is the first on your list. Happiness is doing your "This is it!", not your 'this will do' or 'this will work' but your "This is it!" — the thing in life you really want to be doing that makes you feel great. When you do this, self-confidence becomes automatic.

John Negus is inspired. He makes a living doing what he loves. He is a passionate plant lover and travels the world investigating the gardens and wild flowers of different countries. To John work isn't work at all, it's fun. He's always being asked to write articles for magazines and to give lectures and broadcasts.

John's enthusiasm is utterly contagious when he lectures. Even if flowers don't interest you, by the time John has finished talking you'll *love* them. He describes his walks high in the Alps looking for wild flowers, and his visits to some of the world's famous places like the immaculate gardens of Disney World. When John has shown his slides and talked you through his journey's you leave on a complete high. Is John self-confident? You bet. He's forgotten all about himself by becoming so wrapped up and enthusiastic about what he's doing. John is happy. He has found his "This is it!".

Trusting Yourself Is Second

Trusting yourself is your second step. This step is so important that without it, nothing will change for you. Trust yourself! You're good enough to do what you want. You have a right to be happy.

Trusting yourself takes courage because you need to break away and be yourself. This means saying 'no' to what someone else says you should do.

Believe In Yourself

The problem is you don't always believe in yourself. You don't always believe there's a 'self' inside you worth dedicating yourself to. You feel you're good enough to work for someone else, clean up after someone else and take care of someone else, but not good enough to do your own thing. You are.

Val Pearce trusts herself. Like John she makes a living out of what she loves. Val runs dog kennels in the English countryside. People come from everywhere to kennel their dogs with Val because their pets always return home so happy and rejuvenated.

Both my dogs stay with Val and always return home looking younger and healthier than when they arrived. Val's kennels are more like a health farm for dogs than conventional boarding kennels. They are immaculate. All of her dog boarders sleep out in little chalets and specially built houses, some even have television and radio. Val prepares all the dogs meals herself, and before each dog goes to sleep at night she cuddles each one separately and kisses it good night.

Val is a radiant and happy woman. She loves dogs and loves the countryside. When she reached retirement age it seemed completely natural to start a second career doing what she loved. She trusted herself. In fact it never occurred to her not to. Val has found her "This is it!"

Self-trust is something you gradually develop until it becomes stronger and stronger in you. The easy way to start is so simple that you often overlook it: give yourself permission to be happy. This sounds simple, but without permission self-trust cannot happen. It's the same as if your child came up to you and said, "Mummy, can I have a new paint set?" Until you say yes, your child is going to wait. So are you. Until you say yes to yourself, you're going to stay on the outside of life looking in.

Picturing Your Goals Is Third

Your third step is to picture your goals. Your goal is happiness, how you experience happiness is your "This is it!" You're like a gold mine of happiness and self-confidence right now and could be feeling *great* about yourself. The problem is you don't know how to go for your "This is it!" Your third step will help you discover it and see how to make it happen. This is mental picturing.

Mental picturing is when you relax and picture in your mind the future you want in order to see how to make it happen. It is the easiest and quickest way to achieve your goals. Athletes use mental picturing all the time to win.

The architect Sir Norman Foster was a great mental picturer. Sir Norman grew up in such a poor environment that the idea of studying to become an architect seemed completely impossible to him. But as a young boy he spent hours in his local library reading books and looking at pictures of tall buildings and great cities.

He pictured the buildings *he* would build some day. Sir Norman became so caught up in his dream of designing beautiful buildings that it became an obsession with him. He put himself through school by working nights and went on to create breathtaking buildings all over the world. He became such a respected modern architect that he was awarded a knighthood for his work. Mental picturing provided a key to his future, even though he did it unconsciously at the time. It can for you.

Through mental picturing you can say 'yes' to yourself and make it stick. You can make promises to yourself that you will keep. Most importantly mental picturing will give you the tools to trust and believe in yourself. This technique will back your dreams to the hilt because you will see results immediately.

Failures and insecurities of the past will start to fade away. Success and self-confidence will start to feel natural to you. Soon you'll find yourself in a completely new world. In chapter three you'll learn exactly how to do mental picturing. First let's look at what makes self-confidence up.

It's not good enough for me to say "Take these three steps and you can have self-confidence". You need to look deeper at what self-confidence is and what it isn't. You need to be honest with yourself, face your fear and walk through it. It's much easier than you think. When you do, the happiness and self-confidence that become yours are forever.

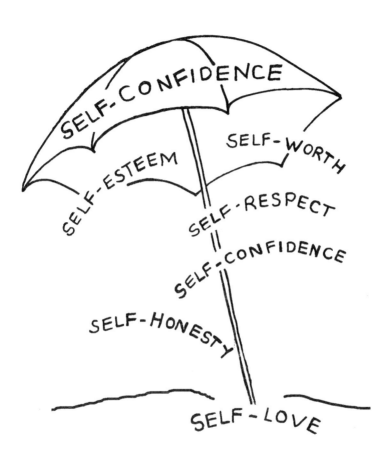

Self-confidence is made of many parts

Chapter Two

Do Your Dream!

So often you're told, "Have more self-confidence!, Value yourself!" or "You need more self-esteem!" The problem is that you don't always know *how*. You think that if you buy something or eat something or drink something you can feel self-confident. This works for a while but soon the high fades.

'Self-confidence' is a general term we use to describe people who are relaxed, successful and self-assured. Yet self-confidence is not just one thing. It is made up of different parts. One of these *is* self-confidence, but there are 3 more. They are self-respect, self-worth and self-esteem. You need them all because when they work together they produce the most valuable 'self-quality' of all which is self-love. When you love yourself something wonderful happens: you become secure.

This sounds idealistic, but it isn't. Self-love is a success quality all successful people share. They believe in themselves. Because they believe in themselves they succeed. You can too.

You Don't Have To Be Perfect

Getting the different parts of self-confidence working together is not difficult. Like anything that doesn't work whether it's a flash light or a car engine, if you take it apart and study it you can see which parts are working and which ones aren't. Then you can fix them.

The good news is, all the parts of self-confidence don't have to work perfectly together in order for you to feel great. They just have to work. Like a car that's a little noisy but gets you to a nice party, your self-confidence just has to get you where you want to go — you can fine tune it as you go along. The other good news is that you can start working on self-confidence anywhere you want. Ask yourself the following:

- If I were self-confident I would start_____?

- What holds my self-confidence back is_____?

- What helps my self-confidence most is_____?

- If I were self-confident I would stop_____?

- If I were self-confident I would try_____?

Problem Solver

These questions will show your strong points. They'll also show where you're blocking yourself. Understanding self-confidence as a separate quality (not a general term) will help you here.

Self-confidence is the problem solver in you. It is the *practical part of you* who can do a job that needs to be done and move on to the next. It's the part of you who can get out of a difficult situation and back on the track. It's the part of you who can pay the bills and if you run out of money knows how to make more so you can pay them. *It is the part of you who can go for it and succeed.*

If you put off doing things to help yourself like looking for a job when you're out of work, cleaning your house or car when they're a mess, writing a report that could land you a good promotion, but instead you binge on food or drink, watch television or spend the day in bed, your self-confidence isn't working.

Self-confidence *solves* problems it doesn't make them worse. Self-confidence says, "I need a new car. This old heap of rust isn't good enough for me any more." If your self-confidence is working, you'll soon be driving a better car. Even if you didn't have the money, you will have found it. Self-confidence gets you to work on time, pays the bills, keeps your life in order and always moves you closer to achieving your goals.

You can't feel self-confidence while you're leaning on someone else for strength. Self-confidence comes from being in control of your life and taking care of yourself. If you feel like a hopeless victim of circumstances you can't feel self-confident, you can only pretend it. But deep down you'll know it's an act. True self-confidence gives you independence and self-respect.

Self-Respect

To have self-respect you need to feel you deserve a good life. In order to feel deserving you need to live with integrity. Integrity means getting what you want in an honest, open way and not at someone else's expense. If you moan, manipulate or steal to get what you want, for example: a promotion at work, a pass on your exam, financial security or a new car, you may get these things but deep down you'll feel ashamed for not getting them in a clean, up-front way that makes them truly yours. Shame poisons your self-respect.

Deep down you know you're a good person, or at least could be. You can't feel like this when you're ashamed. Understanding that you are truly valuable for who you are right now — not because of what you have (or have not) achieved is essential to feeling self-respect. This is an experience in self-worth.

Self-Worth

Self-worth is what you are. Your self-worth can't be harmed. It can't be run over, burned up, drowned or anything like that. No one can take it from you either. You have as much worth as the homeless person begging for pennies — no more no less, but you don't know this about yourself. Some people recognise that they're just as good as the next person but some of us need help to discover this. That's what this book is for.

Imagine you had a rhinestone ring and wore it all the time thinking the stone was worthless. Then one day you took your ring to the jeweller to get it fixed and he told you it was a fine diamond. The fake diamond you thought you were wearing turned out to be a priceless gem. And you had it all the time but didn't recognise it. Well, you're the same. You're like a fine diamond.

Discovering this about yourself is the most valuable discovery you can make. It will show you once and for all that you're valuable and not a fake.

Ask Yourself

- If I felt like a valuable person I would_____?

- If I *really* knew I was valuable, I'd stop_____?

- If I knew I was worthwhile I'd change_____?

- If I knew I couldn't fail, I would try_____?

These questions will show where you are not living up to the best in yourself. Don't be hard on yourself. You sincerely do not realise how much you have to offer. A 'diamond in the rough' doesn't look like much, but when it's polished it's beautiful. Whether a diamond is rough or polished, *it's always a real diamond.* You're the same. *You're the real thing not a fake.* You need to know this about yourself, not hope or believe it but *know* it.

The easiest way to know this is to dive into your "This is it!" — the thing in life you've always wanted to do. Call it your 'dream', your 'buzz', your 'bliss', your 'goal' or your 'heart's desire', whatever you call it, it's what you're here for. It will give you the buzz of self-esteem.

Self-Esteem Creates Beauty

Self-esteem is the *dreamer* in you. It's the *beauty creator* in you that dreams of doing something wonderful with your life. It's the part of you that has something special to offer whether you believe it or not. Getting in touch with this will make you feel so great about yourself that you'll never regret having taken this step.

The way to have self-esteem is to complete your dreams. There is something you can do that no one else can do. There is something you *want* to do that you haven't done yet. We're all looking for something special to do with our lives that has real meaning for us. Something that will inspire us and give us real purpose. This is your happiness — your "This is it!"

Your "This is it!" and self-esteem are the same. You get them from doing one thing: creating beauty. Does this mean painting a 'Mona Lisa' or writing a hit song? No. It means creating something that's beautiful to you. This could be a successful company, a garden, excelling in sports or singing on a stage. It could be *anything* as long as you love it. And it doesn't mean 'making it big' in the eyes of others unless this is what you really want to do. By the same token, if you do want to make it big, don't deny this to yourself.

More Fun Than 'Having Fun'

Doing your "This is it!" will be more fun than 'having fun' because your self-confidence, self-respect, self-worth, self-esteem and self-love will automatically work together. Like the key piece in a jigsaw puzzle, once you find it the other pieces fit neatly into place.

In the past you've tried to impress other people — or compete with them. Now you'll be impressing and competing with *yourself*. It's a real high. You won't have to act self-confident you'll *be* self-confident. You can feel like a million dollars!

You won't get self-esteem by paying the bills, your mortgage, doing the ironing or the dishes. Handling the practical areas of life will give you a feeling of satisfaction and respectability. But everyday tasks, even when you do them well, are not the answer if you want self-esteem.

'Almost It' Is A Stepping Stone

Does this mean you should immediately quit your job or leave school to do your "This is it!" No way. You can't have self-confidence and self-respect when you leave a mess behind. What you're doing right now is a stepping stone that's taking you where you want. Learn as much as you can from it, give as much as you can to it. Succeed as much as possible then move on, *if* you still want to. Very often when we succeed at something and give it all we've got, we don't want to move on. Mental picturing will help you create a seamless strategy for success.

Recognise Yourself

You have a very important need and that is to be recognised for the true person you are. You think you need other people to like you and that's fine. But most importantly you need to like and recognise yourself. You can only recognise yourself through what you do. If you do something worthwhile you will recognise yourself as worthwhile. If you do something hurtful or ugly you will recognise yourself like this.

Deep down you know you deserve more out of life than you have right now. In your heart you know life could be *great* if you could just figure out how to make it work. This is where you get off track by copying (or competing with) others who look successful, happy and have more than you do. It's fine to admire others, but when you mimic them or try to *be* them, you're lost.

What Stops You?

Your biggest block to self-confidence is not trusting yourself. Your critical mind knocks everything you do and makes you give up before you start. It talks in your head saying "That's a stupid idea", "It will never work", "Why bother" or "Don't risk it." Your critical mind can demolish your self-confidence in a flash by convincing you that you never wanted your dream in the first place. Your critical mind tells you 3 things: 1) what you haven't got, 2) that you'll never have what it takes and 3) that if you 'go for it' you'll fail.

It serves one purpose: to make you afraid. See your critical mind for what it is — just fear. Get rid of it by trusting yourself. This is where your third step to self-confidence, mental picturing acts like magic. As you mentally picture the future you want, your enthusiasm and success will automatically silence your critical mind.

Overcoming Fear

Facing fear is an essential step to self-confidence. It is easier than you think. People disagree on what's frightening and what is not, but most agree that fear is the worst thing in the world and that being free of it is best. You may not realise this, but we *choose* fear.

A friend of mine, Ken, enjoys climbing mountains and once described to me his absolute *terror* when he froze on a rock face in the midst of a climb. In that moment he went through all the emotions from dying, to being so injured he was paralysed, letting his family down, being humiliated, jeered at and even annihilated. When he finally managed to crawl up the rock and described to his guide what he had felt, the guide said, "Of course. That's why people climb. The fear is the kick. It's like a drug. The closer to *death* you come, the more *alive* you feel." The problem is that we often seek out fearful situations in order to keep ourselves hyped-up and feeling alive, especially if life gets a little boring.

Fear Of Failure

To become truly fearless, and you can, you need to face your 3 main fears: fear of failure, fear of success and fear of honesty. Let's look at fear of failure. There's a part of you that wants to succeed and achieve the dream you've always said you would do some day but that you keep postponing — the fortune you would like to make, the paintings you would like to paint or the home and family you have always wanted. "Can I make it?" you wonder. Deep down, you don't think so because so far you haven't. Two main things stop you from 'making it'. First, you're not sure about what you really want and second you *are* sure but feel too weak emotionally or physically to go for it. Mental picturing will help you handle both.

Fear Of Success

Once you've discovered your "This is it!" face your fear about achieving it. We fear success because the flip side is failure. We want what we're going for, but fear the responsibility of having it. "The higher they rise the harder they fall" is a cliché, but it's an experience we all dread. Fear of succeeding then falling off the ladder makes us stop before we start. We fall off the ladder either because we get lazy and don't maintain our success or because we barge in unprepared. Mental picturing gives you the tools to plan your success and keep it up. We'll talk about these in the next chapter.

Fear Of Honesty

Last, you fear honesty. This takes 2 forms: honesty about failure and honesty about mediocrity. Let's look at failure first. In our eagerness to get rich quick (admired, loved and so on) we neglect common sense. We try to do too much too fast without planning. We don't pace ourselves physically either. We want the good things of life *now*. We push too hard, get reckless and sabotage our opportunities. Then we fail and decide we're no good. All that's happened is an excess of enthusiasm. You just went too fast. Don't let it brand you for life as a failure. Be compassionate with yourself, but be careful too. Don't *glamourize* your failure and say it was meant to be. Nothing is meant to be but your success and happiness. If you mess up admit it and try again. Turn to page 100 and read about commitment.

Small Start To A Big Adventure

Honestly facing mediocrity is last. Facing mediocrity is impossible for most people, that's why there are few outstanding successes. Often we settle for wanting something instead of having it because we must roll up our sleeves and start from scratch. If you want to build a successful company you have to face that it all starts with making just one sale. If you want to be a singer and all you can do is croak, you need to face this and do what it takes to turn your croak into a tune. If you want to paint beautiful pictures and you can't draw a straight line with a ruler, you have to face this and do what it takes to learn to draw. Go for it! You're not alive to live in the shadows to postpone happiness or avoid getting hurt. You are alive to use your talents to create beauty, success and have what you want. *Having what you want and doing what you want is the only way to conquer fear.*

Trust yourself! You're a fine and valuable person

Chapter Three

The Tools Of Trust

O.K. You're sold. You've decided to choose happiness, trust yourself and go for your "This is it!" How do you get out of a standstill? How do you escape from the frustration of being trapped?

Imagination is the key to changing your life. For better or for worse your imagination is *always* working for you. It's your ability to see life turning out a certain way. Without realising it, we're always using our imagination to rehearse the future.

How often do you say "I knew it!" when something turns out the way you thought it would? How often have you felt "I thought it would turn out that way", or "I had feeling she would say that". You mentally rehearse the future *in advance*. That's fine if you're rehearsing things you want. But too often you are using your imagination to rehearse things you don't want. You go over an incident where someone let you down or hurt your feelings. Or, you mentally argue with someone you don't trust or feel is treating you unfairly. When you have an argument with that person later on you feel upset — never realising you have set the stage.

By using your imagination for worry instead of success your imagination gets into a bad habit. It works against you. You get depressed, lose your self-confidence, give up your dreams and don't know why you feel so let down. The truth is, you're letting yourself down by focussing on failure instead of success.

Get Your Mind On Your Side

The key to self-confidence is to use your imagination to get your mind on your side so you can make the changes you want in life and never look back. The way you do this is through mental picturing.

Mental picturing is where you deliberately picture what you want in your mind's eye in order to see how to make it happen. The East German and Russian athletes made this technique famous when they excelled in the Olympics. It's not only used in sports but in business, health care and education. Trial lawyers always use mental picturing to rehearse their performance before entering the court room. You do the same thing. If you want to ask your boss for a raise or your dad for a loan, you'll rehearse what to say before asking.

Mental picturing is the way you psych yourself up and get in a positive mood so when you do something you succeed. It helps you see life turning out the way you want *before* it happens. It helps you to see circumstances working for you instead of against you.

Natural Courage

Mental picturing is the easiest, quickest way to build self-confidence because it gives you *natural courage.* There is a medically proven reason for this. When you picture yourself as relaxed and confident you bombard your system with 'feel good hormones' called endorphins. By lifting your mood these hormones help you spot opportunities that might have been right under your nose, but that you couldn't see because you were depressed.

When you mentally picture what you want several things happen: 1) you will take a quantum leap in self-confidence and feel great (these are the hormones), 2) you'll start getting ideas about *how* to achieve your goals and 3) things you don't want will start to disappear. Unpleasant things disappear from your life simply because you stop paying attention to them. It's like a friendship that drifts apart when you no longer share the same interests. You and your problems will drift apart when you picture a new lifestyle.

Mental picturing is the most enjoyable way to open doors for yourself. The best part about learning this technique is you'll realise that you had the ability all the time but were just not aware of it. It's like the rhinestone we talked about on page 15 that turns out to be a diamond. You'll realise that you've been sitting on an incredible ability that you've never used, and that you'll always have it.

Three Kinds of Techniques

There are three kinds of mental picturing techniques, those that *create what you want, destroy what you don't want* and *back-up your success*. These techniques are remarkably easy with simple steps. You'll be using long picturing techniques and short ones. They will be real or symbolic. A real technique is something you can actually see yourself doing like driving a new car. A symbolic technique implies the meaning of what you want. For instance 'rolling in clover' or wearing 'gold shoes' implies you have plenty of money. You'll learn these in Chapter 4. Mental picturing works best when you picture scenes that could only occur if you had achieved your goals.

1 Your first step is to *decide*. Make a list of what you want. If you're not sure, list everything you *think* you want and choose 3 more items you're sure about. This could be a new house, a wonderful partner, a healthy body or a huge bank balance.

If the result of being self-confident and successful would be owning a new car, then picture yourself driving this. If it would be losing weight, then picture yourself slimmer. If being confident would mean people congratulating you, then picture this. If you'd dress differently, speak more confidently or have a different hair style, then imagine this. It's fine to have a list of 10 or more items.

2 *Relax* in any way that works for you, just be sure not to fall asleep. Set aside about 15 minutes preferably at the same time each day to completely unwind. Don't think that dedicating relax-time to yourself is being self-indulgent. It isn't. It's an investment in your future. Curl up on your sofa, sit in a chair, stretch out on the grass or take a bath to unwind. A business-person could get to the office early before others arrive and hold their calls. Counting slowly from 20 to 1 until your eyes closed gently all by themselves is a very relaxing way to start mental picturing, breath deeply a few times and then start picturing.

3 Now that you're relaxed, *picture* one at a time each item on your list in a way that implies you *already* have it. Make this scene as vivid as possible, tasting, touching smelling and feeling each scene in 3-D colour and wrap-around-sound if possible. Don't worry if you can't see a clear picture in your mind. All you have to do is imagine what you want as *vividly* as possible. Hearing is a powerful help to picturing. For instance, hear someone telling you how great you look, hear the sound of the sea if that's where you want to live.

4 Once you have pictured your goals, *give yourself permission* to have them. This sounds simple but you won't let yourself have anything without permission. You think you need this from other people. You don't. When you say yes to yourself others will agree. Seal your picturing by saying silently or aloud "I give myself permission to be successful" or "I can have that." Move on to your next picturing technique and do the same.

This scene could be you in a crowd of friends who warmly accept you. If so, when you've finished picturing, say to yourself, "I give myself permission to have a group of friends who think I'm great." Do the same for each item on your list.

5 Come out of your picturing and *affirm* that what you've just pictured is true. This backs up giving yourself permission. Affirmation is a positive, wide-awake statement you make about yourself. For instance, you would say "I John, have a great group of friends", or "I Sue, become more self-confident each day", or "I look and feel great!" Positive affirmations make your picturing *feel real*. They're the icing on the cake and an important part of the process. We will talk more about these on page 125.

6 After you affirm, *act the part*. For example, act like the successful, self-confident person with a great group of friends you just pictured. Dress up! Have you noticed how sales people treat you in stores when you're well dressed? How do they act when you're in sloppy clothes? Research has proven that how you look affects how you feel. When you look at yourself and see a mess, you cancel your positive feelings. The same goes for your house, your car or office. Clean them up as if a successful person used them. Even if you feel like the pits, looking over your clean office, kitchen, car or newly polished shoes will make you feel more positive.

7   *Follow through* on your hunches. The picturing you've done will trigger ideas within your own mind about how to achieve your goals. You may get a hunch to take a night course or join a club. You may suddenly realise how to solve a problem. If you want your picturing to work follow through and act on these ideas. Mental picturing is never a substitute for action, it works hand in hand with action. If you don't act on the positive ideas you get as a result of your picturing you'll achieve mixed results. Some things will work and others won't. If you do act along with your picturing you'll be amazed at how rapidly life changes.

Coincidental Changes

This part of mental picturing is really delightful. Coincidental changes will happen in your life that you just can't explain. When you've been mental picturing, people can spontaneously offer you things and opportunities will crop up that link to your picturing. You may get an invitation to a great party, a trip, a job offer or any number of things. This is the part that people enjoy most about picturing. They just cannot explain some of the opportunities that come their way, except that they've been 'mental picturing'. Take advantage of these opportunities. If you don't, the changes you've been waiting for will not happen.

Ban Disappointment

Disappointment is the greatest form of stress. Getting your hopes up only to be let down can be soul-destroying. If disappointment happens too often it will get the upper hand and you'll start to feel cynical and depressed. These gloomy feelings will wear your health down, reduce your ability to spot opportunities and spoil your relationships. It's medically proven that when you feel gloomy you release stress hormones into your system that make you feel even worse.

Disappointment squanders valuable energy. because when you feel let down you have to boost yourself up. Boosting yourself up by buying things you can't afford, drinking too much or eating too much are last ditch attempts to regain self-confidence. They only make you feel guilty afterwards.

Try Before You Buy

Is your "This it it!" *really* it? Wouldn't you like to know this before you spend a lot of time, energy and money going for it? Mental picturing will help you know this. It lets you try before you buy.

Mental picturing is not 'just going for it'. It's going for your "This is it!" There's a difference. How often have you gone for something tooth and nail only to wind up burnt out, discouraged, broken hearted or broke as you realise "This is *not* it". Mental picturing sidesteps disappointment. As you regularly picture what you want, you'll turn hot on some ideas and cold on others and end up knowing what you really want.

Mental picturing will cut through years of wondering whether a certain job, relationship or place to live is right for you. And it costs you nothing but a little time each day to relax and picture your dreams. For example, if you dream of living on a tropical island picture yourself doing this and you'll soon know if it's just a pipe dream or something that's right for you.

Mental picturing will open any door. But you don't want just any door. You want the one that's perfect for you. Picturing your goals will lead you straight where your heart is. When your heart is in something nothing can stop you. When it isn't, it's an effort just to start.

Your Mind Says Yes

People wonder why mental picturing works so well. This has to do with your mind. There is a part of your mind that says yes to anything you want. It is the part of your mind that is completely on your side. It will take you where you want to go *if* you know how to contact it. This is your subconscious mind and you contact it every time you picture your goals.

Your subconscious is different to your critical mind which never stops harping at you, criticising you or putting you down. Your subconscious mind is your best friend and will never stop helping you achieve your goals.

The problem is you're giving your subconscious messages like "I'm a failure" or "I'll never make it". Research has proven that everything you've pictured and felt up until now has made up your life as you experience it today. By the same token, the mental pictures and feelings you choose for yourself can determine your future.

If you imagine people not liking you or letting you down, you feed messages to your subconscious mind that invite the negative outcome you want to avoid.

Feed your subconscious with positive pictures if you want a new lifestyle.

When Should You Picture?

Practice mental picturing when you have good physical energy, for example in the morning after breakfast. People often picture on the train or bus when they're travelling to work. You can also picture if you're stalled in traffic or waiting for an appointment.

It is important to practice your picturing when you are fresh, before the demands of the day take over your thoughts. If you wake up in the middle of the night this is a great time to picture. You will drop back to sleep easily, sleep soundly and wake up feeling extra refreshed.

Before you go to sleep at night, read your list of goals. Most people are too tired to practice mental picturing before they go to sleep but reading their list and thinking each item over helps them fall asleep feeling 'positively programmed'.

As you drop off to sleep choose one goal to picture. Put your head on the pillow, close your eyes and gently imagine you're where you want to be. Don't make work of this. Just gently fall asleep with this picture in your mind. A client met her husband soon after picturing a ring on her finger each night as she fell asleep.

Steps To Mental Picturing

1. Decide and make a list of what you want.

2. Relax in a quiet place.

3. Picture your goals as if they were already yours.

4. Give yourself permission to have what you want.

5. Affirm that what you've just pictured is true.

6. Act the part of the person you've just pictured.

7. Act on your positive ideas and seize opportunities.

8. Read your list before you go to sleep at night.

Get ready, life is going to take off for you

Chapter Four

Life Takes Off

You'll now learn mental picturing techniques to create the new lifestyle you want. You will learn *realistic* techniques such as owning a new home. You'll also learn *symbolic* techniques that symbolise the attainment of your goals. For example 'Hitting The Jackpot' or 'Rolling In Clover' symbolise having plenty of money. Mix and match these techniques as much as you want. Above all, enjoy your picturing.

Mental picturing is not a 'lying back and letting it happen' scheme. Life will become very exciting and active once you start picturing. You'll start to live a lot more of it! And, boy will you be busy. The good news is that you won't want it any other way. Life is going to take off for you.

Whether you're trapped in a suffocating lifestyle, financial problems, health problems or a dead-end relationship, picturing a new life for yourself will show you the way out. Your confusion will disappear and you'll know clearly what you want and how you want to do it.

A film-maker once said: "I just saw how to do it. Logically, creatively and tangibly. I could see the whole plan of how to achieve my goal laid out in front of me like a road. That gave me such confidence and such certainty that nothing could stop me. But believe me, things started changing so fast that I had to fasten my seat belt!"

Invest In Yourself

You want a new life. You want the best. If you want smart designer clothes, you must value yourself enough to pay for them. It's the same with your life. If you want a great life, you must value yourself enough to invest time and effort into creating it for yourself. The way you invest in yourself is through mental picturing.

Deceiving yourself that you don't have the time for mental picturing, that you're too busy, too tired or don't really care, and that the lifestyle you have now is just fine is fear again. Don't fool yourself, you care. It will help you to go back to page 40 and read about fear.

You want the goal you're picturing but you fear the responsibility of having it. You also fear facing failure in case your picturing doesn't work. You fear letting go of the old life you know because at least you know what to expect of it. The famous opera singer Beverly Sills said "You may be disappointed if you fail, but you are doomed if you don't try." You cannot afford to let fear stop you or you'll stay stuck forever.

Go First Class

Here's a picturing technique that will help you try and and win. Imagine you're smartly dressed and ready to go. You look great with a suitcase in your hand. Walk up to a ticket counter sign posted 'New Life' and buy your ticket, one-way, first class. Imagine an airport, hear the sounds of loud speakers and feel the hustle and bustle.

Hand the ticket attendant your 'Self-Value' credit card. See them writing out the slip and hand it back to you. Sign the slip, take your 'Self Value' credit card back and watch the attendant finish writing out your ticket, put it in it's folder and hand it to you. Take your ticket and walk through the door of the First Class lounge.

Say to yourself, "I give myself permission to have a great new life." Come out of your picturing and affirm, "I deserve the best and *always* travel first class." Now follow through and act on your hunches.

Target Your Techniques

Your lack of self-confidence may be linked to any number of things. Mental picturing for self-confidence is aimed at overcoming your feelings of not being good enough.

You may suffer from a lack of self-confidence because you're struggling with money and can barely make ends meet. In this case being self-confident would be picturing yourself with plenty of money and also picturing how you would spend it.

Picturing yourself driving the new sports car you've bought with your new-found wealth, being popular or being a proficient lover will make you feel much more deserving. When you've finished your picturing follow up on the ideas that will turn your picturing into tangible results. Mental picturing will show you the quickest and easiest way to achieve your goals so you won't waste time or effort on things that don't work.

Become Popular

We all want to be popular and well-liked. Yet you may feel awkward and shy. In this case picture yourself being warmly greeted at parties, being a sought-after guest at smart dinners or giving a successful party of your own. It is especially important to feel the scene you're picturing as if it were real. Feeling is a powerful tool for change. So *feel* the pleasure and self-confidence of being relaxed, at ease and popular. Affirm, "I give myself permission to be well liked and popular."

Get Rich

Several of the following picturing techniques are aimed at having plenty of money. You need enough money so you're not worried about it all the time. Boosting your income through mental picturing always brings a boost in self-confidence. I've never seen anyone use mental picturing who did not substantially boost their income as a result. Many enjoy 'rolling in clover' to get the money flowing.

Roll In Clover

Close your eyes and imagine you are in a field of clover at the height of summer. Imagine you're lying in a field with the sun beating down on you. Smell the clover, feel how soft and lush it is. Now, in your imagination roll around in it. Imagine the clover is like a soft feather bed and that it feels wonderful. Next imagine the smell of clover turning into an overpowering smell of money and feel the thrill of knowing your money problems are solved. Take a deep sigh of relief knowing you don't have to worry about money ever again.

You may wonder how your subconscious mind will be able to tell the difference between the clover you imagine rolling in and the debts you face now. It will. Your subconscious mind is more powerful than any computer. It understands your intentions. Picturing yourself rolling in clover with the intention of becoming financially secure will tell your subconscious exactly what you mean. It will then give you ideas about how to become rich. After rolling in clover say to yourself, "I give myself permission to have more money than I could ever use."

Roll In Bank Notes

You can roll in bank-notes instead of clover. Imagine you're in a huge room rolling on piles of money — wonderful new fresh bank-notes and large gold coins. See the room you're rolling in carpeted with money and rest your head on a mound of money in the corner that works like a pillow. Be sure to have a carry-all with you so you can take as much as you want. Take handfuls of notes and gold coins and fill up your bag. Know that you can come back here whenever you want and take as much money as you want. Say, "I give myself permission to have unlimited money." Affirm, "There is an unlimited supply of money and I can have as much as I want."

Smell Money

Smell the money you're rolling in. Roll around in it, throw it up in the air, catch the money, smell it breathing in deeply then stuff it in your bag. Next, in your imagination take the key to the 'Room Of Money', lock the door and put the key in your pocket. Know you can come back and help yourself whenever you want. Next picture yourself spending the money. Buy what you previously could not afford. Make this scene as vivid as you can and give yourself permission to have all the money you want. Say, "I give myself permission to have masses of money." Then affirm, "I now have huge amounts of money and there's more on the way".

Next, act like a rich person. This doesn't mean buying an expensive new car or clothes unless you're sure it's the right thing to do. Act the part of a wealthy person by acting confident, relaxed and cool — not desperate and needy.

Walk on Money

Another good money technique is to put money in your shoes and walk on it. A £5 note in each shoe works fine. This technique is powerfully symbolic because your feet are your security. You can't feel secure if your feet let you down. If you have so much extra money you can walk on it, even if you're flat broke, your subconscious mind will know what you mean.

People tell me that walking on money makes them feel incredibly lucky. The famous television star Oprah Wimfrey said, "Luck is a matter of preparation meeting opportunity." The way you prepare for opportunity is to programme yourself with positive mental pictures until you feel so lucky you can't lose. As you stride down the street on your £5 notes affirm "I'm a winner". Then say "I give myself permission to have so much money I can walk on it."

Gold Shoes

The motivational speaker Brian Tracy once chided me

for helping others make money and not picturing enough for myself. He said "It is very common for shoe maker's children to go barefoot, you know. Make sure you are not one of them." I had to laugh because at the time, even though Brian didn't know it, my own income was not up to standard. I immediately took his advice and pictured myself wearing gold shoes. I even pictured myself sleeping in them. All of a sudden opportunities came my way that boosted my income. I wasn't doing much differently, except for picturing myself wearing gold shoes. Opportunities sprang up like mushrooms.

Made of Money

You may not think you're made of money, but in your imagination you can be. The more you imagine this the more you'll enjoy it. Close your eyes and imagine you're walking down the street wearing a suit of money. Imagine your suit is made of brand new £20 notes (or £50's or £100's). Feel layers of crisp new back-notes rustle gracefully as you walk. Smell the scent of money waft through the air. Imagine your belt buckle is made of pure gold.

Imagine being this rich. See people step aside for you as you walk down the street. Notice how shopkeepers make a fuss over you when you enter their shops. Say to yourself, "I give myself permission to have so much money I can buy anything."

Mix Socially

Does your lack of self-confidence make you extremely shy in groups of people? So much so that you don't go out socially even though you want to? You can start mixing with people right now in your imagination.

Picture yourself going to a party and being warmly greeted by everyone there. See people shaking your hand, giving you hugs and being happy to see you. See yourself in the middle of a group of people who smile and obviously like you. Picture yourself leaving the party and hear people say "Oh don't go yet. Can't you stay a little longer?" Hear them invite you for another occasion saying, "I'll see you at lunch on Sunday". When you leave, hear people say behind your back, "Isn't he/she such a nice person? So much fun to be with". Feel the pleasure of having had a wonderful time and knowing you're welcome again.

Turn Them Into Rainbows

A rainbow is a powerful symbol of happiness,

fulfilment and everything good. Imagine what life would be like if you had this effect on people? No one would say no to you. The following technique is one I teach to many business people. It never fails. Imagine the minute you meet someone and shake their hand they turn into a beautiful rainbow. Picture all the radiant colours. See a big smile on your rainbow's face.

Use this picturing technique before an important meeting, interview or date. Imagine people reading your business proposal and turning into rainbows as they read because they're so impressed. If you're giving a speech, picture the audience turning into rainbows. Feel the satisfaction of knowing you have a remarkable effect on people. Say "I give myself permission to have a wonderful effect on influential people" then affirm, "I have such a positive effect on people they turn into rainbows."

Walk In Like A Rainbow

A rainbow technique that once worked magic for me was 'walking in like a rainbow'. I had to attend a convention for which I felt completely wrongly dressed. One black suit had to make me look like a million all weekend. There was no time to shop and I didn't know what to do.

I used the airplane flight to picture myself walking into the convention looking like a rainbow and closing sales all over the place. I kept seeing myself walk in like a rainbow and pictured people stop and stare. I even heard 'oohs' and 'aahs' of admiration. I pictured this over and over and *heard* the 'oohs' and 'aahs'. It worked.

My first hunch happened at the airport where I caught sight of myself in a mirror and noticed I needed a hair cut. On checking into the hotel I asked for a pair of scissors and got to work immediately. I cut my hair much shorter and was amazed at how much better it looked. Next I pictured how to dress my suit up with a scarf and jewellery The result was a thoroughly successful convention. I never felt badly dressed, in fact just the reverse and I closed many sales.

Know Your Worth

You are authentic and valuable, not a fake. Believe this by picturing yourself as a diamond. Sit down, close your eyes and imagine you're a diamond. See the stone shine brilliantly. Feel your worth. Make this scene as vivid as you can. You may prefer to imagine you're holding a sparkling diamond in the palm of your hand and that its brilliance is shining around you and filling the room. Know this diamond belongs to you. Affirm "I am a fine diamond and nothing can take away my worth".

Adapt this technique to suit yourself by picturing an emerald, sapphire, ruby or a big pile of gold. The important thing is to experience yourself as authentic and valuable — not a fake.

Priceless

On page 15 a rhinestone turns out to be a diamond. This is an example of undiscovered worth. Picture this now as if it's *really* happening so you can *experience* your own worth. Relax and picture yourself walking into a jeweller's to get your 'rhinestone' fixed. See the jeweller glace at your ring, discuss the repair, then stop and take a closer look. See him look at you and *hear* him say, "That's a very fine diamond you're wearing. May I examine it closely?" Take your ring off, watch him examine it through his glass and turn to you with an astonished look on his face saying, "This is one of the finest diamonds I have ever seen. It's a fine, beautiful stone worth a great deal of money. If you ever want to sell it, please let me know."

Imagine how you'd feel if this really happened to you. All the time you believed you owned a fake diamond, and suddenly learned you possessed a gem of incredible value. Such value in fact, that it could wipe out your financial worries and keep you in 'clover' for the rest of your life. Capture the feeling of new-found wealth.

The diamond technique is a symbolic way of impressing your subconscious mind. The diamond symbolises you. Your subconscious mind will help you realise how valuable you are. Give it a chance. This may happen in many ways. Someone may thank you for a job well done and say "I don't know what we would have done without you". Or you may feel stronger physically, have increased mental clarity or finally tell someone who's been making you miserable to shove off.

Eating Out Of Your Hand

One of the greatest blocks to self-confidence is feeling out of control or that other people are withholding what you need. You want them to see things your way, but it's hard going. They just don't understand.

There are several short picturing techniques that will help you gain influence and control. A really enjoyable one is seeing people 'eat out of your hand'. Close your eyes and imagine your boss, your husband, or your mother-in-law is eating out of your hand because they're so impressed with you.

If you have ever fed sugar cubes to a horse you'll know the feeling of how this enormous animal eats gently out of your hand. Feel the horse's muzzle in the palm of your hand as it eats up the sugar cubes. Feel the gentleness of its muzzle, hear it crunch the cubes. Other people in your life can act like this. They can be gentle, kind, powerful, considerate and 'eat out of your hand'. All you have to do it picture this. Be sure to feel the *pleasure* of knowing people like you so much they ate out of your hand.

Open Doors

Another effective picturing technique for getting accepted, particularly in the business world is to see doors opening for you. Picture your goal. This could be a career change that gets you out of a boring job into an exciting one. It could be a brand new house that gets you out of a bad neighbourhood into a good one. It could be a passing mark on your exam that get you into college.

Now see doors opening for you one after the other. These can be golden doors. Or, large important polished wood doors with shiny plaques inscribed 'New Job', 'Manager' or 'College Graduate'. Picture the door of your choice open for you and see people on the other side waiting for you and smiling. Feel them shaking your hand as you enter. Enjoy the pleasure of finally being where you really belong.

You may want to picture social doors opening. Imagine you're being welcomed by the kind of people you want to be with. These can be artistic people, aristocrats, rock stars, young kids or anyone that suits you. You have a right to choose your friends. As a last touch, walk through 'new doors' into a golden light. Many business people like this one. Light symbolises happiness, success and peace of mind.

Creating a new life is easy when you picture it first

Mental picturing makes life more romantic

Chapter Five

Self-Confidence & Sex-Appeal

What's one big reason you relax for half an hour every day and picture your goals? Firstly, you want to change your life and achieve new goals. But there's something more. That something more is appeal. Namely sex appeal. We all want to feel desirable, when we don't we feel life is passing us by.

You cannot live an exciting life on the outside unless you live an exciting life on the inside. Mental picturing helps you live magically. When you find your "This is it!" you'll feel so great about yourself that you won't be needy any more. This gives you a lot of sex appeal. You won't have to *act* sexy you will *be* sexy.

I've never taught mental picturing to anyone, of any age, who did not develop increased sex appeal as a result. In fact becoming too attractive to the opposite sex became a happy problem. Men find that suddenly a lot of women are interested in them, and women experience the same with men. This makes life a lot more fun.

If you lack self-confidence you probably don't feel people are attracted to you. You may not feel you have have any sex appeal either. Yet some of the so-called 'ugliest' people have immense sex appeal. The movie actor Humphrey Boghart was not considered handsome in the classical sense yet he had incredible sex appeal to millions of women. Men the world over tried to imitate him. What was his secret? He had a magnetic aura that made him immensely appealing. You will too if you start picturing regularly.

You'll develop a magnetic aura that no one can really define. People will want to be around you and touch you. This quality is known as charisma and you'll develop it. The reason for this is simple: you will have become emotionally self-sufficient. You won't feel needy anymore because you'll be supplying yourself with success and happiness. You'll enjoy your own company and not feel dependent on others. This turns other people on.

Fall In Love With Yourself

Mental picturing will spark up your love life. You'll be *living* an exciting life instead of watching it. You will get rid of your grudges against other people because you'll be doing what you enjoy and achieving your own goals more easily. Making things happen for yourself gives you a feeling of independence and power. Sex appeal will be automatic.

You develop sex appeal because you start to succeed. Opportunities you have been waiting for will start to fall into place. You will have found the golden key to making your life work and others are going to want to know your secret. What really happens when you start mental picturing is that *you fall in love with yourself* and others follow your lead.

The following picturing techniques are designed to give you added sex appeal and liven up your love life. They will be equally effective in any arena, be it business or personal. First a word about sex.

Don't Settle For Sex

Don't settle for sex. Make love instead. Sex is most satisfying and pleasurable when carried out in a loving relationship. When you care for, and are deeply attracted to your partner, making love can lead to passion — the missing ingredient in most people's lives. People who experience real passion know it's incredible. There is no drug or drink that can substitute for this feeling.

If you haven't yet experienced real passion you owe it to yourself to try. You'll become 'hooked' and far from making you go on the prowl real passion will make you very selective about sex. It's like fine food: when you have had the best, imitations will no longer do. The following picturing techniques are designed to help you replace sex with wonderful love making. Some techniques may make you laugh, but they will add sparkle to your sex life. Love making should not only be passionate, it should be a lot of fun.

Many techniques include images of fire and heat. This is because fire is a powerful subconscious symbol for warmth, responsiveness and passion, whereas ice symbolises frigidity, inability to respond or impotence.

Irresistible

A great picturing technique for increased sex appeal is to imagine you are wearing a T-shirt with the word 'Irresistible' written on it. Meet your date, walk into a meeting, or down the street picturing the word 'Irresistible' on your chest and see what happens. You'll feel attractive, lucky and special. Picturing yourself as irresistible can even change your posture. I learned how powerful the 'Irresistible' technique was when I taught mental picturing to a business woman. She was extremely competent at her job but did not feel attractive to men. She didn't think she had any sex appeal at all. She decided to try the technique. After a short time she got a promotion at work. Up until then she had been struggling against the glass ceiling and could rise no further in her career.

She was delighted at how her picturing techniques were opening doors for her at work. They were also making her surprisingly attractive to the opposite sex. Several men became interested in her, two of whom became jealous of one another. Both proposed marriage. Today she is married, thriving in her career and is expecting her first child. She was no longer considered 'young' when she started her 'irresistible' picturing, so it's never too late.

A Message From The Myths

Mythology, in particular the Goddess Aphrodite, can teach you a lot about love making. Aphrodite wore a magic girdle that made everyone fall in love with its wearer. The other goddesses always wanted to borrow Aphrodite's girdle, but she rarely lent it them. Naturally she wanted everyone to fall in love with her.

Wouldn't you? In your imagination you can borrow Aphrodite's girdle.

Picture a beautiful low-slung belt made of spun silver and gold. See Aphrodite walk up and give it to you and then put it on. Feel how it clings to your hips and then close your eyes and imagine you are 'Irresistible'. Before you come out of your picturing technique say, "I give myself permission to have people fall in love with me". Affirm, "People just can't help falling in love with me".

Make Love To A Tiger

Maybe you wish your partner was more of a tiger in bed or that *you* could be more like one. In your imagination you can both become tigers. It will certainly add a lot of sparkle to your love life.

Making love to a tiger is a symbolic technique which goes like this: imagine an intimate scene with your partner, such as supper, but instead of seeing your partner as you know them, picture them as a tiger instead. Hear your 'tiger' give a low roar of desire and then embrace you. Run your hands over your tiger's smooth fur and powerful body. Add to this scene as much as you want. Before coming out of your picturing say, "I give myself permission to be a tiger in bed." then affirm, "I am so sexy I am a tiger".

You can vary this technique by picturing yourself with 'Tiger' written on your chest like the 'Irresistible' T-shirt technique. You can also picture yourself as a real live tiger with fur and powerful build as you walk down the street or snuggle under the covers. Affirm "Being a tiger in bed is great fun". Don't be surprised if you get an urge to visit the zoo to see the tigers. People who picture tiger scenes want to do this, and more.

Become A Hot Ticket

A 'Hot Ticket' is someone who is really sexy. You can become a 'Hot Ticket' too. Picture a ticket in your hand with your name written on it. The next time you go on a date, or meet someone you like a lot, sit down and do some picturing first. See yourself handing him or her a 'Hot Ticket'. You could picture something like 'Dave's Hot Ticket' or 'June's Hot Ticket'.

Picture your partner stunned with delight as they take the ticket from you, eyes wide open. Then see your partner look at you with intense desire and imagine you're both being engulfed in flames of passion. Add to this by *hearing* the sound of a huge crackling fire. Feel the warmth of the fire and imagine it surrounding and enveloping you both until there is only the sound of the blaze left.

This will do it. Don't worry, you won't cause a fire except one inside you. This is a symbolic technique to generate passion and your subconscious mind will know exactly what it means. Before you come out of your picturing say to yourself, "I give myself permission to be powerfully passionate". Then affirm "I'm a 'Hot Ticket'. No one can resist me" and follow up on your hunches. Don't be surprised if you get an idea to throw an intimate dinner party, buy special underwear or watch romantic videos. Go for it: your subconscious mind knows exactly what will turn you *and* your partner on, so follow your hunches.

A Hunk

"Whew! What a hunk!", or "He's a real hunk." How often do women say this to describe a really attractive man? You can become a hunk too. Picture yourself walking into a party and know you look great. Hear a hushed silence as you enter the room and see heads turn.

Notice one stunningly beautiful girl in the crowd, the kind of girl every man dreams of. See her turn and look at you with recognition, as if she has been waiting for you for a long time. Then watch her walk over to you and introduce herself, stammering a little because she finds you so attractive. Leave the party together and as you walk out, overhear other women saying, "Isn't he good looking? What a hunk!" Before you come out of your picturing, say "I give myself permission to be a hunk". Then affirm, "I am so attractive girls can't resist me".

This is a good technique to picture before you go to a party. Modify it to suit your needs. Be sure that as you're getting ready to go out you look in the mirror and say 'I'm a hunk.' Picture the word 'Hunk' written on your chest.

Straight-Laced?

A lot of people have been brought up in such conservative environments that their inhibitions hold them back. If inhibitions stop you from enjoying sex, looking at it another way will help. Do you have trouble enjoying a pizza, or a piece of chocolate cake? Probably not. Enjoying sex should be no different. You should be able to throw yourself into love making and enjoy it just as much as these delicious treats. Mental picturing will help you do this. You learn everything. Few babies like their first taste of pizza or chocolate cake, but little by little they learn how delicious these are. Soon all they have to do is just see a piece of pizza or cake and their mouth waters. You can learn to respond like this to sex.

Straight-laced people aren't much fun, and making love should be fun. A good picturing technique to get rid of your inhibitions is to picture yourself wearing a pair of shoes that lace up tight on your feet and ankles. You often see these shoes in westerns. You can take off these restricting shoes that symbolise your inhibitions.

Picture unlacing these shoes, taking them off and throwing them on a bonfire. Watch your constricting straight-laced shoes burn up. Or, picture your partner doing it for you. Put your foot on your partner's knee and watch him or her unlace your shoes and throw them away. Then imagine powerful passion overtaking you both.

Thaw Out

Another great picturing technique for getting rid of

inhibitions is seeing an ice cube melt. Picture an ice cube with your name written on it (or your partner's) and then picture it melting. You can put your ice cube in front of a roaring fire, or melt it with a hair drier to speed things up. Then affirm, "I am completely thawed-out and passionate".

If feeling passion is difficult for you, read a book or watch a movie you find romantic. Imagine you are the hero or heroine in the romantic scenes. Your subconscious mind will know exactly why you're reading the book and picturing this way and will produce the results you want.

Say to your self "I give myself permission to enjoy making love and to let go of all my inhibitions." *Why not? What have you got to lose but loneliness?* (It goes without saying you should practice safe sex.) When you come out of your picturing affirm, "I am free and uninhibited and can fully enjoy sex."

Now act relaxed and self-confident about sex. It won't be difficult. As you take off your straight laced shoes and burn them up or thaw out your ice cube, you will start feeling differently. You'll be much more relaxed and find you respond more easily to the opposite sex.

Mouth-Watering

The following picturing technique will not only make you desirable, it is a great for closing sales. I have never seen it fail. Picture your prospective partner *salivating* with desire! As dogs watch their supper being prepared they just can't help it. The dinner looks so delicious and smells so great they can't control themselves. Their mouth waters and they drool.

In your imagination picture yourself meeting your partner. See them look at you with a face full of admiration and wonder. Then see them start to salivate uncontrollably because they find you so attractive. Watch them stumble on their words as they try to speak to you because they find you so irresistible. Picture them simply salivating with so much desire they're speechless.

As a next scene, imagine you and your partner are making passionate love. Hear your partner say "I can't live without you". Before you come out of your picturing say, "I give myself permission to be irresistibly attractive to the opposite sex" then affirm, "I'm so irresistible I'm mouth watering". Now, act as if you're attractive instead of down and out.

Fall Asleep Feeling Sexy

One of the best times to use mental picturing for more sex appeal is around bed time. The reason for this is because you're very relaxed and in clear contact with your subconscious mind. Just before you drop off to sleep imagine the word 'Sexy' written on your chest or your night clothes. Dropping off to sleep *feeling* sexy is one of the best things you can do to increase self-confidence and sex appeal.

Close your eyes and as you drift off *feel* that you're sexy and irresistible. Imagine what life would be like if you were this way. Affirm silently "I am sexy and irresistible" or "People fall in love with me easily". If you wake up in the middle of the night, use this time to do a little picturing. You can imagine you are a bonfire of passion. Or, picture yourself as a tiger, sexy, or even 'edible'. Then go back to sleep and see how you feel in the morning. You may be surprised at how your mood changes. Picturing in the night will make you feel extra self-confident the next day.

Sprinkle Star Dust

The following technique is guaranteed to add sparkle

to any relationship. Sprinkle star dust on it. If you and your partner have been together for some time, your relationship may need some renewing. When making love becomes routine it loses its sparkle.

A technique both men and women enjoy is sprinkling star dust. Picture yourself sitting with your partner, then in your imagination sprinkle star dust on the scene. You may want to first picture your partner then sprinkle sparkle dust all over their shoulders and hair. This is a great technique for relationships that are basically sound but getting a little dull. Affirm, "My relationship is better than ever and now has extra sparkle".

Give a Gift

When a relationship is magical there is nothing like it. The two of you together just sizzle with fun, laughter and desire. In one of my other books I describe a gift-giving technique for business negotiations. This technique is great for giving magic to a relationship. You may have just met someone you want to really impress. Or maybe you're interested in making your present relationship more intimate. Giving your partner a gift of magic can work wonders.

Relax, close your eyes and imagine you're giving your partner a beautifully wrapped gift. This can be a huge box or something tiny and precious. See your partner open their gift and beam with delight because you've given them exactly what they want. You can put little gift tags on your package that say 'Intimacy', 'Passion' or 'Laughter'. Write on the gift tag whatever your relationship needs most.

A Ring On Your Finger

The symbol of a ring on your finger is a powerful one. It means you belong to someone and someone belongs to you. If you practice the following technique consistently you can't fail to attract the right partner. You may attract a few 'dress rehearsal' partners first, but eventually the right one will appear.

Imagine a wedding ring on your finger. Some people buy themselves a special ring to wear that helps them feel this is true. Your ring doesn't have to look like a wedding ring but you'll know what it means. Each night as you fall asleep feel the ring on your finger and feel the happiness of being together with the partner of your dreams. Affirm, "I am now married to the partner of my dreams and we are very, very happy." Whether you marry in the legal sense is less important than feeling you're married in your hearts. Add to this technique by picturing yourself in a garden with your own children. Women often picture holding the baby they've always wanted in their arms.

Feel The Scene

With all picturing techniques, whether they're for making love, closing sales or getting well, it's important to *feel* the scene you're picturing. Feel the confidence of being attractive, successful and desirable and then to the best of your ability act the part. The picturing techniques in this chapter are specially designed to make you feel more desirable.

If you are having trouble responding sexually or are losing interest in sex a visit to your doctor can bring surprising relief. You may have become over-tired or be suffering from the kind of mild depression that a simple course of vitamins could remedy. If you have sexual problems it's a huge relief to talk them through with a sympathetic professional. There's nothing like a listening ear when you need one.

Your mind will give you anything you want

Destroying depression brings pure relief

Chapter Six

Destroy What You Don't Want

As you use mental picturing to create the future you want, use it also to destroy what you don't want. Destroy mental attitudes like depression, financial problems like being in debt, or health problems. To confidently start opening doors for yourself you must get rid of what's holding you back. This chapter focuses on negative character traits and attitudes that dampen your self-confidence. You may not even have these traits, but if you believe you do, they'll damage your self-confidence.

Using mental picturing for destroying things may sound negative, but the only things you destroy are problems you'll *never miss*. Techniques that destroy are some of the healthiest you can do. When you mentally picture getting rid of anger, you'll be amazed at how relaxed, reasonable and serene you feel. Don't take my word for it. Try it.

You Need Will-Power

Scenes that help you let go of the past will clear your negative moods. Make these scenes as vivid as possible if you're depressed or struggling with rejection. These take more effort and will power than your other picturing. It's worth it. Negative feelings slow you down. Getting rid of them puts you back in control.

Many find having a cup of coffee before a picturing session boosts them up when they're down. You can even have a glass of wine. But try to limit it to a glass or 2 because if you drink a lot of wine and then have a great picturing session it can end in a hangover. Your picturing may be a terrific success, but the after effects of a hangover will cancel your positive feelings.

Depression Is First On Your List

You can't feel self-confident when you're depressed. If you feel like a failure, ugly or stupid, your attitude will change very quickly through mental picturing. Even when you've felt like this for years.

Depression must go. Depression is sadness and feeling cut off and left out of life. Depression can *paralyse* you, but believe it or not mental picturing will shift this negative mood in no time. There is no pill on the market that will act so fast to give you a 'natural high'. It has been medically proven that picturing positive future goals releases beneficial hormones into your system. These enhance your mood in a natural way that alcohol, smoking or drugs cannot do. Try it.

One main cause of depression is the feeling trapped in a lifestyle you don't want to be in but feel powerless to change. You want happiness, peace of mind and a sense of purpose, but life seems empty. Start asking yourself what you would do if you weren't depressed? Would you be rich? Famous? Good looking? Would you live somewhere different to where you live now? Ask yourself the following:

- If I were rid of depression I would_____?

- If I wasn't depressed I would stop _____?

- If I weren't depressed I would dress in_____?

A creative approach to depression, like picturing positive future goals works better if you get rid of your anger first. Destroying anger or depression through mental picturing is a *pleasure*. Remember, mental picturing techniques that destroy will not destroy anything real. You can't destroy a sunset or a starry night. However these beautiful views, just like your happy future can get covered over by dark clouds of depression. You can clear the view.

Dynamite

Close your eyes and picture a building, for example an old warehouse with the words 'Anger' or 'Depression' written on it. Imagine you're holding a cable with several sticks of dynamite attached to the other end that are placed inside the building.

You may enjoy putting the dynamite there yourself. If so, walk up to your 'Anger Building' with several sticks of dynamite in your hand which have a cable connected to them. Place the dynamite inside the building then walk back to the plunger box. Take a good look at your 'Anger Building' and push the plunger. Watch the building explode and enjoy how great it feels. Affirm "Anger, you're history. If you try to come back, remember I have a *ton* of dynamite".

It helps to practice this technique over and over because suppressed anger is poison to your system. It's impossible to feel relaxed and confident when you're eaten alive by anger. It also makes life very tiring. You may not realise why you're so tired, but keeping a lid on your anger takes enormous effort.

However, when you express anger in a clean, safe way, as you do through mental picturing, it's pure relief. It brings a feeling of control and satisfaction that you're doing something constructive about your anger. You can destroy a boss who is making you miserable or even that tax man without a fight. Techniques like these always bring positive results.

Beat It Out

Another way of dealing with anger is to mentally picture while you're doing something. A friend of mine beats on her bed with a piece of hose when she feels angry and frustrated, usually at her noisy neighbours. When she's finished beating the bed and her anger's spent, she can face her neighbours in a friendly way and ask them to "keep it down". She says beating the bed has often saved her from an ugly argument when she feels ready to fly off the handle. Getting rid of anger is key to beating depression. With depression gone, you'll feel like a different person.

Get Rid Of Your Ball And Chain

Do you feel because of your past you can't do certain things? That you can't succeed because it's too late? Or because you don't have the education? Perhaps you're self-conscious of your family background or because you've gone bankrupt and don't feel you deserve another chance. It's never too late. The past does little but remind you of how and when you've failed.

You can be free of the past. This is one way to do it: imagine there's a ball and chain locked to your ankle. See the word 'Past' written on the ball. Picture this ball as enormous with a huge heavy chain. Reach into your pocket, take out a key and unlock the chain from your leg. Roll the ball and chain of the 'Past' over a cliff or toss it in a garbage truck and toss the key in after. Turn around and walk into the future where there's sunlight, a pile of money, a good looking partner, a sunrise or a rainbow. You can add to this scene in any way you wish. The future you want is waiting for you once you've dumped your past.

Erase Rejection

Rejection is part of life, but boy does it hurt when you don't know mental picturing. Even with mental picturing you'll experience rejections but they won't get you down. Rejection is just one door closing so another one will open. You'll know this when you start picturing regularly and experience the success it brings.

The following technique relieves the sting of rejection. Close your eyes and imagine the word 'Rejection' written on a piece of paper in pencil. Erase this word and write the word, 'Acceptance', 'Fame', 'Desired' 'Loved' or whatever you want *in ink*. Open your eyes and say "Rejection and set backs no longer affect me because I'm going for my "This is it!"

Dump Your Fear

Depression and fear go hand in hand. Our greatest fears are of being trapped and not having control. Get out of the trap of fear by dumping it in a rubbish bin. Write a list of everything that makes you afraid. Write down every last fear, large or small. It could be fear of losing your job, money, or health. Next write down the people you are afraid of and why. These could be your difficult father, your boss or the police. Last, write down past experiences that have made you afraid. When you've written down every person, memory or thing that makes you afraid, crumple the list up and throw it in the rubbish bin.

You may prefer writing these fears on bits of paper, crumpling them up one by one and then dropping them in the rubbish. Next, in your imagination tie the bag of rubbish up tightly and put it out for the bin men to collect. Picture the word 'Fear' written on the bag, and see the rubbish men pick the bag up, toss it in their truck and grind it to pieces as they drive off. Affirm "My fear is gone and will never come back."

You can also explode your fears with dynamite. Or you may prefer to burn up your list of fears when you've finished writing them. You can do this in your imagination or in reality. Just do it safely. You may need to repeat this technique several times to feel free. Do it often. Eventually, writing the same fears over and over and getting rid of them will make them seem harmless. You'll start to feel free. You may not believe this is possible, but if you practice these techniques, you'll see.

Break The Chain

Now that you've dealt with depression and anger, you can zap situations you feel trapped in. You may be involved in a chain of events over which you have no control. You could be trying to close a sale, get a project started, find a job in a slow market or end a relationship. You may feel that because of outside pressures you can't do anything. Break the chain of events and you can get moving. This is how it is done.

Picture a large heavy chain and imagine you're a strong person like the television hero, The Incredible Hulk. Pick up the chain in your imagination, feel your muscles expand with powerful strength and pull the chain apart. You may be surprised at how easily it comes apart. The chain you thought was unbreakable simply *bends open*. In your imagination throw one part of the chain off to the right and the other off to the left. Then walk forward. You're no longer 'trapped in a chain'. Go where you want. If you prefer, dump your chain in the rubbish, throw it off a cliff or bury it. When you've finished, say "I give myself permission to break this *ridiculous* chain of events."

Get Rid Of The Mob

Fear and panic are terrible. They undermine your self-confidence as nothing else does. When you have a panic attack you feel desperate. It's as if a mob of voices is inside your head all shouting at once. Outwardly you try to appear composed and relaxed but inside you're tied up in knots. The more you try to appear calm, the more tense you become. You make a superhuman effort to relax at an interview or social occasion but when it's over you go home and collapse, exhausted.

Panic and fear happen when you're in conflict. You try to make a good impression but your critical mind harps at you: "You shouldn't have said that", "You should have left a bigger tip", "You shouldn't have come", "They're bored with you", "You're wasting your time." This mob of voices must go.

Try this: relax and picture an angry mob all shouting at once. The mob represents your critical mind. Next, as if by magic, see the angry mob disperse, become quiet and walk off in different directions. See the place they've left become silent. I like to picture Trafalgar Square in London late at night for this. I silence my mob until there's not a soul left in sight. This impressive and magnificent square becomes completely silent and deserted. I picture this to quell panic and it works. Vary this technique by seeing your angry mob turn into *gentle lambs*. Picturing people turn into lambs helps handle aggression or lack of cooperation.

Rip It Off

I learned another fear technique when my back was against the wall. I had to catch an international flight after working with a client. The snag was that I had exactly two hours to get to the airport — a drive that would normally take three hours in good traffic. Neither the client nor the flight could wait.

I left my client's office on a Friday afternoon which is the worst time to travel. Roads are always jammed with people setting off for the weekend. Panicky about missing the flight, I drove as fast as possible and pictured all the way. Firstly I pictured myself arriving at the airport *early*, and kept affirming, "The drive was so quick and easy that I got there early".

The next thing I did was to picture a magic board, the kind that children draw on. This magic board has a sticky cardboard back covered with a clear plastic that can be pulled up. When kids draw on it, pictures appear because the plastic sticks to the backing. When they pull the plastic up the picture disappears as it unsticks and there's a fresh surface to draw on. I kept picturing the magic board with 'Fear' and 'Panic' written on it. Then in my imagination I pulled up the plastic (I *heard* it rip off the sticky backing) and wrote 'Serenity', 'Peace' and 'Arriving Early' in their place. It worked. The traffic was unbelievably clear that day and I arrived at the airport even earlier than imagined. There was plenty of time for a much needed meal and drink. It felt wonderful.

Pull The Plug On Failure

Nothing shakes self-confidence like failure. We talk about this on page 21. When you fail or barely scrape by you feel dreadful. Memories of failure must go or when you try again your mind will be occupied with previous failures. When this happens, succeeding is almost impossible, or at best a struggle. There's nothing in life you can't learn, and learning to succeed through mental picturing is fun. The more you succeed the more self-confident you'll feel. *Ultimately, succeeding is the only way to develop sound self-confidence.*

A great picturing technique is to wash off failure in the bath. You may enjoy buying a special 'Success Sponge' and some great smelling soap to go with it. When you bathe, take your Success Sponge, soap it up and wash failure off of every inch of your body. Work up a wonderful lather and rinse off well. Then pull the plug on 'failure' and watch it go down the drain with the bath water! Affirm, "Failure is now out of my life." An added bonus is that you'll sleep soundly after sudsing-up technique like this in the evening.

Look Great

Do you feel ugly in some way? Do you have a physical

or emotional defect that makes you feel unattractive? Even though others don't see you as ugly, (they may even see you as good looking), you think you're unattractive. Feeling ugly poisons self-confidence. You need to get rid of this feeling. Erasing works well for this or any negative trait you want out of your life.

Close your eyes and picture a piece of paper with the word 'Ugly' written *in pencil*. In your imagination erase this word. Then take an imaginary pen and write the word 'Great-looking' or 'Beautiful' in its place *in ink*. Erasing a word written in pencil and re-writing another *in ink* is a powerful symbol to your subconscious mind. A word written in pencil can be *erased*. A word written in ink is *permanent*. Now act as if you're so attractive you're irresistible. People tell me this picturing technique makes them feel especially attractive to the opposite sex. You can also replace the word 'Ugly' with 'Warm', 'Loving' and so on.

Techniques that destroy will get rid of anything you don't want. The next chapter explains how to ensure that your picturing techniques will work. You'll learn how to back up your success.

Back up techniques are mental good luck charms

Chapter Seven

Back Up Your Success

So far you've learned 2 kinds of mental picturing techniques, those that create what you want and destroy what you don't want. Now you'll learn a third technique which is to back up your success. These are short winning images that symbolise success. Do them at the end of your picturing session, or during the day when you're in the mood. If you're waiting at the dentist's, picture some. Or if you're stalled in traffic, do some back-up techniques until the traffic moves.

These short techniques take about twenty seconds each and you can practice them over and over. If you're pressed for time and can't carry out your normal picturing routine, back up techniques are great stop gaps. They encompass a feeling of overall success and act like 'insurance' to help your other techniques work.

Hit the Bull's-Eye

Hitting a bull's-eye is an excellent back-up technique. It symbolises irreversible success. It's very effective for helping you with your timing. Timing is incredibly important in everything you do. If you do the right thing at the right time you'll always succeed. If you do the right thing at the wrong time, you won't. Getting your timing right is essential if you want to succeed.

Close your eyes and imagine you're an archer, shooting a bow and arrow. Pull the arrow back and picture the target. Picture a word in the middle of the bull's-eye, such as 'Self-Confidence', 'Self-Esteem', 'Admiration', 'Closed-Sale' or whatever you want. Feel the tension in the bow as you pull the arrow back and then in your imagination release the arrow and let it fly. See it hit the bull's-eye and *hear* it thud. Feel the satisfaction of knowing you've 'hit the bull's-eye'. Come out of your picturing and affirm, "My timing is perfect and I always succeed". Use the arrow technique for anything you want. The next technique men relate to as well as women.

Bloom

Blooming like a flower will help your self-confidence. Blooming symbolises growing into maturity and completion. It also implies fulfillment and recognition. Relax, close your eyes and imagine you're a flower bud.

It can be any kind you choose: a rose, a poppy, an orchid or a daisy. See a perfect fresh bud and then, as if you were watching a film, see this bud open gracefully to become a beautiful full-blown flower. Smell the fragrance and see others admire it. Be sure to admire it yourself. Picture the loveliest flower you can imagine. Capture the feeling that you're really like this. Come out of your picturing and say "I give myself permission to blossom and be admired".

As The Crow Flies

Are you getting delayed? Are you running around in circles only to end up in a blind alley? Picturing a direct route for yourself will trigger ideas that will lead directly to your goal. One way to do this is to picture a crow fly. Going forward 'as the crow flies' symbolises the shortest, most direct route to arrive where you want. Crows are known to fly *straight* to their food and shelter. They never get lost. You don't have to either.

Close your eyes and imagine you're a crow. Or picture your crow from a distance the way a bird watcher would. Your crow can have your name printed on its chest in gold or on its wings. See the crow spread it's wings and fly directly to its nest in picturesque surroundings. Picture the bird settle in, close its eyes, and go to sleep with a big grin on its face.

Flying like a crow, or seeing your name on a crow as it flies *directly* to its nest and settles in, sets you up for an easy completion to your goals. If the crow's black colour bothers you, picture a gold crow instead. See it land in a golden nest. It's your imagination, use it to picture any way you want. When you come out of your picturing, say "I give myself permission to achieve my goals directly and without delay".

Over The Moon

Everyone knows that 'over the moon' means you're happy. Life is going your way. Picturing yourself over the moon will give you a real boost in self-confidence. Practice this technique in one of two ways. Firstly picture a moon and then imagine you're flying over it the way Peter Pan would. Capture the feeling of flying through a dark night studded with stars and illuminated with a huge full moon. Experience your feeling of wonder as you fly 'over the moon'. Affirm, "I'm over the moon with happiness".

Second, imagine you're standing looking at a full moon on a clear night. Feel the magic of the night as if the moon has given you a gift. Next, imagine you're really *over* the moon. Find yourself looking down on a luminous full moon below you. Imagine you're right on top of it. Stand on it! This technique is designed to make you feel you're singled out for good luck. Picture it before a meeting, a date or dropping off to sleep. Or, go for a walk on a moonlit night, gaze at the moon and imagine you're a star shooting over it.

Make An Entrance

On page 48 I describe a technique called 'Mix Socially'. Making an entrance is a similar technique for feeling accepted and well liked. Imagine you're entering a room where a crowd of people are gathered. Hear the buzz of friendly conversation as you walk in, then see everyone turn around and smile at you. You may enjoy seeing people come up and shake your hand or even bow to you. All of these actions symbolise you're well-liked, respected and an addition to a social gathering.

Seeing people bow to you or 'bending over backwards' are especially powerful symbols to your subconscious mind. These actions convey respect and carry a strong message that you make a difference. If you don't feel you count, this technique will make you feel more valuable. Be sure to feel the relaxed self-confidence of knowing you really belong. Remembering a time when you felt this way will help. It doesn't matter if this was as far back as childhood. Your picturing will be more powerful if you superimpose a memory of when you felt confident and positive.

Giant Peanuts

Do you feel you're dismissed by people you want to impress as if you're 'just peanuts'. Why not become an impressive peanut everyone will notice? Close your eyes and picture a peanut with your name written on it. See the person you've been trying to impress (or group of people) with their backs turned. Then imagine your 'peanut' grows to a giant size. See people turn around and stare with bulging eyes at the 'peanut' they turned their backs on. See them look astonished and then watch their faces turn *green* with envy. They turned their back on this peanut, and now look how impressive it's become!

Picture yourself as a peanut growing from small to large or picture yourself as a peanut made of pure gold. See people gulp and gape, saying 'oohs' and 'aahs' of admiration. Come out of your picturing and feel the satisfaction of knowing you're finally recognised. Say "I give myself permission to make such a positive impression that people are speechless". Affirm "I make a difference".

Small Potatoes

'Small Potatoes' means the same as 'Peanuts'. You're not much. You can be dismissed and ignored. Wrong. Small potatoes is effective and fun to picture because your subconscious mind will interpret a small potato that turns into a large one with power and recognition.

People may treat you as if you're just 'Small Potatoes', but you can astonish everyone including yourself by becoming the biggest potato on earth. Picture a scene similar to that of the peanut but as a potato instead. Imagine a little tiny potato that grows into a huge golden potato with your name written on it. Next see people ogling it, pointing and talking amongst themselves. Be sure to feel your own astonishment at seeing a huge golden potato and knowing it's you. Add an extra touch by imagining the potato has grown so large it's become the planet.

Don't worry, you won't turn into a peanut or a potato by picturing these techniques. You'll begin to feel more worthwhile and people should treat you with more respect. If you develop a craving to eat potatoes or peanuts, take it as a sign that your picturing is working.

On Top Of The World

If you see life as something you need to fight your way through instead of a journey to be enjoyed, it will be a struggle. Seeing life as a friend is essential to self-confidence.

One of my clients sees life supporting her by picturing herself 'on top of the world'. She pictures laying on top of a large rock by the sea only she imagines the rock is the planet instead. As she imagines herself stretched out on this rock with the sun shining down she affirms, "Life totally supports me in everything I do".

When she goes to the theatre she imagines life is supporting her there too. When the audience applauds she imagines they're clapping for her. She affirms silently to herself, "Life is great and everyone supports me". These techniques combine visual images as well as sound. By picturing them your general attitude to life and other people will improve. As a result people will help you much more.

Ace Update

In my book **You Can Have What You Want** I describe a back up technique called acing a serve. It's always exciting to ace a serve when you play tennis. You win the point in one shot with no opportunity of a comeback from your opponent. This is a no-turning-back image that helps you feel like a winner.

One of my readers described an amusing experience he had after he was picturing acing serves to help close several sales he'd been working on. He closed quite a few sales but what delighted him most was what it did for his tennis game. He was an average player, but after picturing himself acing serves, he aced one serve after another. He had never done this in his life. His partner was amazed and wanted to know *how* he had improved so much, so fast. My friend assured him that he'd only been picturing acing serves not practising in secret.

Choose the road of self-esteem

Chapter Eight

Going Forward

Expect plenty of change when you start mental picturing. Doors of opportunity will fly open. Other times life will stall or even go haywire. Don't worry! When things are great, you're going forward. When things are chaotic, you're *still* going forward. For example, if you've been picturing for a new career and suddenly the company you've been working for goes bankrupt and you're out of a job, hang in there, your picturing is working.

Stepping Stones

What seems like a negative event is forcing you to find a better job so you can move up in the world. We unconsciously force changes on ourselves that will get us moving. Most of the time these changes will be as exciting as anything, other times they can be uncomfortable. They're always a stepping stone to success. I tell clients who start mental picturing, "Treat everything that happens to you from now on as a stepping stone. Even if it seems negative it's helping you go where you really belong." It always does.

Two Skeletons In A Cave

To go forward with mental picturing you need commitment. Commitment takes courage. It is your willingness to live up to the best in yourself and let your 'poor me' go. It is your determination to do what is necessary to succeed and achieve your goals. Commitment and courage go hand in hand.

I learned about commitment when my son told me a joke. He said: "Mom, two skeletons were sitting in a cave. What did one skeleton say to the other skeleton?" When I couldn't figure out the answer he said, "If we had any *guts* we'd get out of here." That joke changed our life. I realised my own fear was keeping us trapped in a demoralising lifestyle. I'd gone through a divorce, was out of work and we were living in a depressing little flat. I had to change my commitments fast.

I decided to set up my own business, something I had been thinking about but was afraid to try. Almost overnight we had moved to a new home in a neighbourhood that was ideal for my son and convenient to me. My business thrived and we never looked back. What did it? I committed to a better life. In one moment of total honesty I admitted I was 'gutless' and was settling for second best. Something neither my son nor I deserved. Self-honesty changed my commitments. I decided to go for my "This is it!" and not just talk about it. It took courage but it succeeded. In fact going for it turned out to be much easier than staying trapped. I was never trapped in anything but my own fear.

You're Committed

You may not realise it, but you're already committed 100 per cent of the time. But to what? Are you committed to doing what you really want? Or are you doing what someone says is right for you? Are you committed to what will bring you deep happiness? Or are you waiting for someone to deliver this to you? Depending on what you're committed to your life will be full and successful or disappointing and empty.

If you don't know what you're committed to, it is easy to find out. Look at what gets your time, energy and money and you'll know what you're committed to. If you are living a great life congratulate yourself. You have positive commitments. If you're trapped and depressed your commitments are negative and you're not valuing yourself. *Everything* you have in life right now is what you are committed to, whether this be wealth or poverty, health or illness, happiness or sadness, too much work or not enough. Some of your commitments may be positive, some negative and need changing. Through mental picturing you can change almost anything.

Professionals & Amateurs

Completing what you start is the key to commitment. It will develop a strong sense of self-worth in you. All successful people are compulsive completers. When they say they're going to do something they do it, no matter what it takes. When they give their word they keep it. If for some reason they can't, they explain *in advance* why. The difference between amateurs and professionals in life is that professionals keep their word. Amateurs break it.

Become a professional. Keep your word with yourself. How many projects do you start and let drop? How often do you break your word? Become a professional. Keep your word with other people and with yourself. If you say you are going to telephone someone, do it. If you tell yourself you are going to do something, do it. You may not realise it but up until now you may have been committed to *wanting* instead of *having*.

One of my readers wrote to me saying, "I used to spend hours watching soap operas on television and drooling over the dresses the stars wore. One day I stunned myself by thinking out loud 'Do you want to watch this or do you want to have it?' I realised that if I wanted the good things in life I had to give them to myself and not wait for someone to give them to me".

A Way Out

Completing what you start strengthens self-respect. You've done what you said you would do and trust yourself as a result. Even if this is cleaning out your garage, it will give you a buzz of accomplishment.

Does this mean you have to complete everything you start? No. For most of us, finding our "This is it!" is a matter of trial and error. It is the height of wisdom to let go of downers whether this be a demoralising relationship, career or lifestyle. Do it nicely if possible.

If you've had it with your job, start creating a way out by looking for a new one instead of fighting with your co-workers until you get sacked. If your partnership just won't work, talk it through so you can stay friends. If you're hitting the bottle, value yourself enough to stop. Your time and energy are much better spent on activities that bring out the best in you.

Out Of The Cave

The skeletons in the cave can help you escape from depressing commitments. Imagine you're one of those skeletons my son described sitting in a cave. It's cold, wet and drafty. You're shivering with cold and your teeth are chattering. You're thinking, "I wish I had the guts... I wish I had the guts..."

Next, in your imagination look down and see 'Guts' written on your stomach in big letters or even neon lights. Feel real guts in the pit of your stomach. Take a deep breath of courage. Feel a surge of pride and resolve of knowing you finally have the guts to do your "This is it!" Feel your body warm up and your teeth stop chattering. Then get up, imagine powerful energy is filling your body as you stride out of your cave with purpose. Feel your strength grow and grow. Look down at your body (which before was nothing but bones) and see how fit and good-looking you've become. Picture yourself striding confidently into life — the career, relationship or new home you want. Feel the satisfaction of knowing you've left that depressing cave forever. Affirm, "I give myself permission to let go of fear and to commit to the lifestyle I want."

A Time To Dream & A Time To Do

Self-confidence comes through achievement. If you spend hours gossiping over lunch with friends or in front of television watching the life you'd like to be living, be honest. You're not committed to living, you're committed to watching. Don't be hard on yourself about this. You're not ready to dive into life yet. You will be. There is a time to dream and a time to do. When you are ready to do your "This is it!" you'll know it and nothing can stand in your way. You'll have better things to do.

Get Off the Roller-Coaster

Getting off the roller-coaster and walking through the 'Happiness Door' will help you dive into life. Close your eyes and imagine you're on a roller-coaster and that you're *not* enjoying the ride. See the words 'Useless Delay' written on the side of the roller-coaster. When it comes to a stop get off and let the others continue. Walk away from the roller-coaster into a door with a gold plaque marked 'Happiness'. Affirm "I've stopped delaying happiness and now go for my "This is it!"

Smooth Sailing

A picturing technique that can help you discover your "This is it!" with a minimum of effort is 'Smooth Sailing'. Imagine you're sailing a boat headed for the "This is it!" pier. Feel the warm sun shining and a fresh wind in your face and blowing your hair. Experience the smooth, steady sailing of your craft. See the sun sparkle on clear water. As you come close to your destination, see people waiting with champagne at the "This is it!" pier. Step out of your boat to be warmly greeted all around. Affirm, "Finding my 'This is it!' has never been so easy. It was all smooth sailing."

Now, follow through and act on your hunches. After 'Smooth Sailing' you may get an idea to take a night course or a part time job that supplements your income. Not all the things you picture will turn out the way you expect. Even if you experience a set-back, don't let it stop you. By acting on your hunches you'll develop a spirit of adventure that will be great fun. You'll realise perhaps for the first time, that life is on your side. You'll attract opportunity like a magnet.

Written In Stone

We associate the written word with fact so writing your

successes in a special note book each day will help you stay determined and confident. Your successes can be simple in the eyes of others but important to you. For example a big success could be building up courage to make an important telephone call you've been putting off. It could be asking someone you like for a date. Your success could be finally figuring out how to solve a problem. It could be saying 'no' to someone you're fed up with. Successes are anything that help you become stronger, more confident and let go of fear. You'll know what they are.

A success journal is a great anti-depressant. When you're down you forget you've succeeded. Your journal is *living proof* that you have. It will remind you exactly how, when and where you've already succeeded and that you can do it again. Your journal is private. It's for your eyes only. So are your picturing techniques. Share these only with people you can trust to encourage you and then sparingly.

Hit the Jackpot

Hitting the jackpot is a sure-fire picturing technique to bring you good luck. Close your eyes and imagine you're playing a one-armed-bandit gambling machine or a fruit machine at a fun fair. Imagine you hit the jackpot! Hear the bells go off, sirens sound and see money pour all over the place. Picture yourself inundated in a sea of money. See crowds gather saying 'ooh' and 'aah'. Picture the game master offer you more prizes – gift-wrapped boxes, silver dishes and *more money*. Imagine driving home in your car piled high with prizes and overflowing with money. Feel the thrill of hitting the jackpot and know you can do it again.

Procrastination Is O.K.

Procrastination can be invaluable if you know how to use it. There are two kinds of procrastination, negative and creative. Negative procrastination stops you from accomplishing your important goals. If you spend hours on the telephone talking to friends about your illness, your hurt feelings or your unfaithful lover you are into negative procrastination.

Creative procrastination is your friend. This is when you put off the trivia of life: the ironing, the paperwork and routine chores and do something challenging that brings a huge reward. For example, you need to write a report that could land you a big sale but your car is a mess and needs cleaning. Forget the car and write the report. You will feel better when you make that sale. You can hire someone to clean your car. Perhaps you dream of doing something creative. In that case do it. If you've painted a beautiful picture, who cares if the dishes get cleared?

Get Rid of Time Wasters

Make time for special things, don't wait for it to be given to you. Analyse how you're spending your time right now, then take time away from something that can wait and spend it on something that rewards you. Even if you only make a small start, like taking one lesson in painting, or working out once a week in the gym, or reading for fifteen minutes a day on a new subject that interests you. Little by little, these new activities will become part of your life. Eventually they become a big part. Don't wait for all or nothing or you'll wait forever. Ask yourself some questions:

- If I had more time I would_____?

- If I spent less time on _____ I could?

- The reason I can't do _____ is?

Watch For Burn Out

Once you discover your "This is it!" there will be no stopping you. You will want to learn, do and be so much that you can become obsessed. You will want to spend every waking moment achieving your dream. You can become very over-worked because you're doing so much, so fast.

Watch your sleep, and be sure you get enough. Drink plenty of water and keep an eye on your diet. Eat plenty of good food, even if you get a little over-weight it doesn't matter, you need the energy. Try not to live too much on coffee, other stimulants, drinks or sweets. These won't hurt you once in a while, like a celebration when you drink wine or eat chocolates after a productive day. You'll feel you deserve a treat.

Nonetheless, burning out when you're racing to achieve your "This is it!" spoils the fun. If you're burning out or teetering on the edge, see your doctor or someone who can get you back on your feet. It is the height of wisdom to get professional help when you need it. This is not a sign of weakness, it is a sign of strength. The right help at the right time will speed your "This is it!" Delaying getting help can bring you to an abrupt halt.

You may need to see a doctor or a therapist. You may even benefit from learning to meditate. Massage, aromatherapy or a high energy diet may help you get strong again. Getting help should not be considered an expense, but an investment in your future.

Audio Tapes

Some of the best help these days comes in the form of self-help audio tapes. These tapes are unmatched if you're looking for a new direction. They offer an excellent alternative to therapy because they're convenient and reasonably priced. Turn on a tape and you can have your own 'therapy session at home'.

Self-help tapes usually offer 2 approaches: motivation and relaxation. Motivational tapes offer confidence building talks on business skills, health, good looks, relationships, self-confidence, goal setting and so on. Relaxation tapes are designed to help you deeply relax and unwind. They're superb stress tools and offer some of the best meditations going. If you're worried or wake up in the middle of the night, play a tape to get back to sleep. You can even play tapes continuously while you sleep. If you elect for therapy, good self-help audio tapes will accelerate it.

Counselling

Counselling can be an enormous help when you're going through a crisis. Psychotherapy is one option. It's aimed at helping you understand why you're in difficulties. It focuses mainly on your past in order to get to the root of your self-defeating patterns, such as depression, phobias and fear.

Don't feel self-conscious about getting therapy. Top business people, doctors and nurses have therapists to help them through rough patches. Professional help can provide a real turning point. There is nothing like a listening ear when you need one.

Coaching in Mental Picturing

One-to-one training in mental picturing is success coaching not therapy. It focuses on your future and will, in a remarkably short time, help you find your "This is it!" It is a very solution-orientated approach to accelerated goal attainment. It will not ignore your problems, but view them as stepping stones to opportunity.

You first identify your goals. Don't worry if you don't know exactly what you want. That's why people elect for this coaching. Finding your "This is it!" then becomes the goal. You'll pinpoint the hurdles preventing you from achieving your goals. On your own you'll practice tailor-made picturing techniques to remove these barriers and speed your progress. You'll experience positive results immediately.

You need three sessions. When you've finished your third you will have mastered the technique of mental picturing in such a way that you can apply it to any situation, any time, any where. You will have learned how to read your own mind. Business people find that learning mental picturing provides them with a seamless transition to peak performance. One of my clients said, "It's the difference between buying a suit off the rack and going to Saville Row and having one tailor made."

Relaxation

Meditation is fast becoming a relaxation technique. It's *not* a religion. Top business people use it to cope with heavy work loads and too little sleep. Teenagers find it helps them feel relaxed and confident around other people. It will improve the quality of your attitude, but not the quality of your life unless you combine it with mental picturing. I always suggest that people use it as a mental picturing tool. Every time you meditate you contact your subconscious mind. Once you're relaxed start picturing your goals and you'll *print* these pictures in your subconscious mind. When that happens the positive outcome you want is only a matter of time.

Many doctors recommend meditation for people who are under stress. This technique has 2 goals: to quieten your mind and reduce fear so you can experience a sense of stillness and peace. Once you have experienced this you're never quite the same again. Life's stress and turmoil will lose its power over you.

Pampering

If you are stressed, tense, in pain and all knotted up, massage and facials can relax you enormously. Men experience as much benefit from facials as women. By relaxing the face, you relax the mind and with it your entire body. When you're physically relaxed everything works better. There are numerous therapies like flotation, aromatherapy and massage of every kind. You may think spending money to pamper yourself is an extra. It isn't. Investing in your own well-being pays huge dividends by helping you relax and think clearly. When you're relaxed you make the right decisions.

Get Out Of Burnout

If you have been burning the candle at both ends, you can burn out. A simple yet effective picturing technique for getting out of burn-out is to picture a candle lying on its side and burning at both ends. In your imagination, pick up the candle and stick the bottom end firmly in a candle-holder or dish so that the flame at the wrong ends goes out. Hold the candle until the wax is dry and set firmly in place. Stand back and admire your candle. See the flame at the right end burn brighter and brighter, stronger and stronger. Imagine smelling a scented candle or see your candle turn into a powerful Olympic Flame. Know it represents you.

Picturing a candle flame will give you ideas about how to get out of burn-out. It will also increase your physical energy. The flame technique is also great when you're confused and need to think clearly. A candle flame is a universal symbol for clarity and vision. When you finish picturing affirm, "I am a bright flame that can never be extinguished".

Happiness is doing what you love

Chapter Nine

The Butterfly Of Happiness

Inside you there's a joyful, creative, enthusiastic person. This person cannot live with disappointment. Like two people who don't get along, disappointment and happiness can't live side by side. They fight, get depressed and ill. You need to connect with the happy person inside you. This Imaginary Journey will help you do that. It will help you rediscover that you have one purpose in life and that is to be happy. It will show you how to find the happiness you've been seeking.

Read through this Journey In Imagination slowly. It's a meditation and is written in a different style to the rest of this book in order to lull you into a dreamy state. Many images are *repeated* several times so that your imagination can create as many sights sounds, scents and colours as possible. If you picture scenes that are different to those in this Journey that's fine. Let your imagination take you where it wants. Above all, enjoy the experience.

You can record this Journey using your own voice in order to get a deeper experience. Or you can order a

117

pre-recorded version combining deeply relaxing sound and imagery from Touchstone Publications.

The name of this Journey In Imagination is The Butterfly Of Happiness. It is said that happiness is like a butterfly and that when you chase after it, it will always be just beyond your grasp. But if you become quiet and still it will fly down and alight on you. And that is what you are going to do in this journey. You are going to become quiet and still.

Remember, this is your Journey In Imagination and the purpose of this journey is for you to discover your happiness. Because happiness is not something you think through, or logically work out, it's something you feel. It's something you discover within yourself. There is something that you can do that will bring you profound joy. There is something you can do, that no one else can do that will fill you with happiness. And that is what this journey is for. To help you discover what it is.

In order to get the most out of this journey, to really enjoy it, you may want to sink into a soft chair, and put your feet up, take a couple of deep breaths and allow yourself to fully relax. It's a wonderful feeling to begin to relax. Allow the relaxation to begin moving through your body. Let it move into your feet, relaxing them completely and then your ankles and calves, and next relax your knees, then your thighs. Feel the relaxation moving into your abdominal region and then gently filling your chest and arms, and then your shoulders and back. Let the sense of relaxation overtake you as it moves up into your neck and into your head, relaxing your forehead, your cheeks, your jaws, the muscles around your mouth and your eyelids. Feel your whole body begin to relax with a blissful sense of stillness and peace.

Happiness is doing what you love, and it's never too late to start. There are many things that can bring you a sense of satisfaction and pleasure. There's companionship, having a home of your own, a good job, health and respectability. All these things can bring you real satisfaction, but there is something that you can do, that no one else can do — some activity that will bring you profound joy. And while you may not know what it is right now, you can discover it.

Imagine that you are starting your Journey In Imagination and that you are at the edge of a wood on a warm spring day. The leaves are just beginning to come into bud on the trees and the dry leaves from winter are still on the ground forming a soft carpet as you walk. The sun is glinting through the trees and you can hear the sound of birds echoing back and forth through the wood. You hear the sound of a river close by as it splashes over the rocks. You begin walking into the wood, and as you walk a feeling of expectancy and hope wells up in you, because you're walking on a path of happiness — your path of happiness — and by following it you're going to discover the happiness you've been seeking.

So walk along this pathway now, and discover your happiness. Walk along this pathway and enjoy the day, feel the warm breeze blowing and hear the sounds of the wood, and the soft padding of your feet on the leaves. And hear the sound of leaves as they rustle in the breeze. As you walk along, you come to a sunlit clearing in the wood, and you begin to feel dreamy and drowsy. You experience an overwhelming desire that you can't really explain to sit down and relax. With the sun filtering down through the trees, and the soft breeze blowing, and the sounds of the wood, you find a big tree and you sit down, leaning your back against the trunk, and you loose yourself in reverie, in a daydream...

Your mind begins to wander and you dream and you dream, and you explore. As you sit here, leaning your back against the tree, lost in your daydreams, you realise that you can have almost anything you want and that there are so many possibilities open to you. In fact, it's almost difficult to choose because there are so many things you can do and have and be. Yet there's one thing in particular that will bring you profound joy, something you can do that will bring you more happiness than anything else.

And as you sit here wondering what it is, something catches your eye, and you notice that a beautiful butterfly has been floating around you, gently dipping and diving. You realise that it's been here for some time, and you wonder for how long? You sit very still so as not to disturb the butterfly or frighten it away. You sit and watch the butterfly dip and dive and float gently around you with wings of radiant colour. Sitting very still, you feel almost hypnotised by its beauty. And before you know it the butterfly floats down and settles gently on your hand.

You gaze at this butterfly in a sense of wonder as you watch its wings gently open and close, reflecting the light in radiant colours. Wings that are delicate yet strong. The butterfly that has settled on your hand is your butterfly of happiness, it's here just for you. It has a message for you. Gently the butterfly lifts off from your hand and begins to fly around you, and you understand that it wants to tell you something. You intuitively understand that this butterfly wants to communicate with you. It may want you to follow it to a place where it will show you something, or it may want you to fly with it. Go ahead! This is your imaginary journey and you can go wherever you want. So go with your butterfly and discover your happiness. Let it show you the way. Follow your butterfly. Let it show you the way.

As you walk in the wood your butterfly once again flies down and settles on your hand, and in your heart of hearts, you know what you are experiencing is true. Happiness is doing what you love and it's never too late to start. It's only too late to wait, because when you're happy, you make everyone else happy too. When you're happy you heal your body and you heal your emotions. You let go of the past and creating beauty becomes second nature to you.

There is something that you can do with your life that will bring you that happiness. Something that will fill your emptiness and your butterfly is showing you what it is. It's showing you how to start bringing the happiness you want into your life.

Soon, you're going to go back to the place where you started your journey, and you'll part with your butterfly for now, but it won't leave you. In fact, it will always be here for you, ready to meet you. Any time you want you can come back and take this Journey In Imagination again and again, to meet your butterfly of happiness and clarify your direction, to re-commit to what you want or just to be together.

Soon you will find that you're back, close to the place where you started your journey, and you become aware once more of the sound of the birds in the trees and of a soft breeze blowing. It's as if you'd been in a timeless place with your butterfly, but now you feel happy to be back, relaxed and full of inspiration and new resolve; ready to begin living and to start making a life out of the happiness and fulfilment that will be yours. What you experienced in this journey in imagination can be yours. To get the most benefit out of this journey, read it as often as you want. You may enjoy writing down the high points you experience: the visual images, the sounds, your feelings and thoughts. You can then picture these regularly to start bringing the happiness you want into your life. *This and other books and tapes by Julia Hastings can be ordered from Touchstone Publications, P. O. Box 57, Haslemere, Surrey GU27 2RW*

Positive self-talk keeps you committed

Chapter Ten

Keep It Up!

Affirmations are statements you make about yourself, other people or about life. When they're negative like "I'm stupid", "I'm dumb", or "I'm ugly", they undermine your self-confidence. When affirmations are positive, like "I really handled that well" or "I'm great!" or "I'm good-looking" they give you a boost.

Affirming positive statements about yourself, others or about life keeps your mind on your side. Positive statements have an immediate effect on your conscious mind. It's the same as if someone came up to you and said "Gosh, you look wonderful!" Even if you felt awful, hearing this would make you feel better. You might think "Well, maybe I don't look so bad after all". This is exactly how affirmations affect you. They help you take a second look at yourself.

When repeated, affirmations sink into your subconscious mind and produce a permanent change of mood. Say them often enough with mental picturing and you can't go wrong. You'll experience a change of attitude that nothing will reverse.

Three Good Things

One of the best affirmations you can do is to pick 3 good things you've accomplished each day and acknowledge these. People often do this as they travel home from work. Instead of berating themselves for what they haven't done or the work still untouched, they think through the day and acknowledge 3 good things they've accomplished. This puts them in a positive mood and helps them leave the office behind. When they arrive home, instead of being preoccupied with unfinished work they're able to relax.

If you're a housewife or are working from home affirming 3 good things is essential when you finish your day. Because like a turtle who carries its home on it back, your office is always with you. At the end of the day when there's still so much to do, call a halt and acknowledge 3 accomplishments, like ironing the shirts, writing an important letter or changing the beds and you'll feel more positive. As most people know, particularly women, anyone who can do this much in a day is doing a lot.

The Mechanics

Affirmations are icing on the cake. They complete

your mental picturing. Think them, say them out loud, listen to them on audio tape, or write them in a journal. After you've taken a Journey In Imagination affirm, "I'm successful and happy", " I'm doing my dream and feel great!" or "Nothing can stop me".

When you're getting ready for work, look in the mirror and say "I'm a winner". When you travel to work say, "This is going to be a great day". Affirmations are fun to say as you wash the dishes or take a walk. Saying affirmations will help you act the part of the confident person you're becoming. They'll also trigger ideas about how to become successful.

In the previous chapter we talked about writing your successes. The same goes for affirmations. We associate the written word with fact so writing your affirmations in a special book can make them feel more real. You might write, "I, Sue, have a happy marriage and beautiful home" or "I, John, am a sought after artist".

Say and write only the affirmations that feel right to you. Using the wrong affirmation is like wearing a colour that doesn't suit you. The following affirmations give you some examples. Make up many more of your own.

Happiness

My life is full of opportunities for happiness.

Happiness is doing what I love.

Putting off happiness serves no worthwhile purpose.

I have one purpose in life and that is to be happy.

Doing my "This is it!" gives me a happy buzz.

Trust

The more I trust myself the more self-confident I am.

The more I do my "This is it!" the more I trust life.

One of my main goals is to completely trust myself.

I trust myself by being honest about what I really want.

I trust my dreams and my ability to make them happen.

"This is it"

Doing my "This is it!" is what I'm here for.

Doing my "This is it!" is more fun than having fun.

My "This is it!" is exciting and never, *ever* boring.

When I'm doing my "This is it!" life has purpose.

Doing my "This is it!" is coming home.

Success

The more I succeed, the more self-confident I become.

When I do what I enjoy I succeed easily.

I always succeed.

Succeeding is the ultimate high.

Succeeding is much easier than being trapped in fear.

Commitment

My most important commitment is to be true to myself.

Committing to my happiness contributes to everyone.

Self-sacrifice is worthless and I now let it go.

Committing to myself is more fun than drifting.

I commit to the talented and valuable person I am.

Self-Esteem

My self-esteem grows daily.

I have self-esteem because I create beauty in life.

I value myself because I create beauty.

The more beauty I create the happier I become.

I'm proud of myself and have let go of shame.

Purpose and Goals

Happiness is my single most important goal.

My purpose is to succeed not fail.

My goals are perfectly suited to me so I succeed.

I have let go of the time wasters in my life.

When I follow my purpose life opens up for me.

Life

Life supports me. Failure, illness and poverty do not.

I use my talents to create a great life for myself.

I've stopped delaying my dream and feel wholly alive.

The more I do my dreams, the more life works for me.

Life is on my side.

Coaching In Mental Picturing

One-to-one coaching in mental picturing is geared at high-achievers. It is also useful for those who are ready to make the leap into a fuller career or more committed personal lifestyle.

Mental picturing first became known in sports when the East German and Russian athletes used it to excel in the Olympics. Golfers and skiers are known mental picturers. This technique is now being used in business, health care and education. The use of mental picturing to accelerate the attainment of goals is unparalleled.

You Are Always Picturing

"How often do you say "I knew it!" when something turns out the way you thought it would? Without realising it you are rehearsing an event *before* it happens. This is mental picturing."
You Can Have What You Want © Julia Hastings

The problem is that we often picture the events that we worry might happen instead of using our imagination to shape the events we want to have happen. Mental picturing will teach you how to do this. It will give you the tools to achieve a seamless transition to peak performance. To contact Julia about one-to-one coaching or workshops, see page 135.

Other Books And Tapes By Julia Hastings

Julia Hastings specialises in teaching mental picturing. Her books and tapes have been translated into several foreign languages. Books and tapes do not repeat each other, but work hand-in-hand as powerful tools for change.

Book - You Can Have What You Want, beautifully designed with 10 full paged cartoons shows you how to succeed in relationships, money and health. "You don't have to settle for second best, you can have what you want." This book will show you how. £4.99

Tape - Your New Self Image co-ordinates with **You Can Have What You Want.** Your self-image is what you think you are. It's also what you feel others think about you. Side 1 explains mental picturing. On side 2 you'll take a relaxing Journey In Imagination and change your self-image for the new one you want. 60 min. £7.99

Tape - The Butterfly of Happiness co-ordinates with **You're Great!** Happiness is like a butterfly. If you chase after it, it will always be just beyond your grasp. But if you become quiet and still, it will fly down and alight on you. On side 1 you'll learn how happiness is doing what you love. If you don't know what you want, the Journey In Imagination on side 2 will help you find out. 55 min £7.99

Tape - Self-Confidence, Self-Esteem & Self-Worth, *You Need Them All!* This single cassette is one of Julia's most popular tapes and is an excellent third tape to go with **You're Great!** You're often told, "Be more self-confident! Have more self esteem!" But what makes these up? In a group workshop Julia discusses the aspects of self-confidence and tells an inspiring story of healing. 60 min £7.99.

Book - The Day Dream Diet, *The Inner Game Of Dieting* will turn your into the good looking person you should be. Rejuvenate, shape up and create a great future through mental picturing. This book will help you succeed on any diet or get the upper hand on eating disorders. It's 'Silver Bullets' diet and beauty secrets work like *magic.* Contains the latest information on mind-body chemistry, picturing techniques, case histories and over 20 cartoons. You'll meet 'The Fat Monster' and get him out of your life forever. £8.99

Tape - Creating Your Own Future. double audio tapes co-ordinate with **The Day Dream Diet**. We often feel our future is predetermined or that a heavy hand of fate is holding us back. Don't believe it! Side 1 & 2 discuss the 3 essential steps to creating your own future. Side 3 & 4 take you on a deep, relaxing Journey In Imagination where you will choose your ideal future. Because many use 'The Journey' for better sleep and to manage stress, it has been recorded on both sides to save re-winding. 115 min. £15.99.

Contacting Julia Hastings

Julia is always happy to hear from you. Her books and tapes are available at good book stores or by mail order from **Touchstone Publications**. If you would like to contact Julia directly, order books, tapes or receive information about seminars and one-to-one coaching write to:

Touchstone Publications,
P. O. Box 57, Haslemere, Surrey,
GU27 2RW, England,
EMail Address
106562.410@compuserve.com

Other Helpful Resources

The Site,

This Internet site offers comprehensive information for young people (of all ages) who want to explore the huge range of career opportunities available to them as they approach the end of school and move on through their late teens and early 20's. While geared towards the young, this is an *excellent* resource for anyone wanting to learn a new skill. If you've decided on your "This is it!" The Site will give you advice and contacts on how to get training. Internet address www.thesite.org.uk. The book, **Go For It!** by Martyn Lewis, lists all The Site's information in book form. Available at good book stores or through Lennard Publishing, Harpenden Herts., Al5 5DR. £8.99

Dr. Jeremy Russell,

Paulton's Square Practice, 5 Paulton's Square, London, SW3 5AS, Tel: (0171) 352 6464, or 352 5172. Dr. Jeremy Russell, is a doctor with a listening ear. His solutions are often so simple that his patients wonder why they waited so long to get help. The practice offers the best medical service along with psychotherapy, psychiatry, physiotherapy and aromatherapy all under one roof. Non-NHS.

The British Register for Complementary Practitioners, P.O.Box 194, London, SE16 1QZ. This charitable organisation supplies free names and addresses of registered practitioners in every category of counselling, massage, reflexology, aromatherapy etc. Send approximately 50p worth of stamps on a large SAE and tell them what you need.

Friend's Meeting House, Friend's House, Euston Road, London NW1 2DJ, (0171) 387 3601, offer meetings and meditations all over the world. Ask for the Friends House nearest you that offers a 'silent' meeting so you can learn how to meditate. The Westminster Meeting House in London is known for this. I learned to meditate there as an aid to mental picturing. A non-denominational organisation with a green slant, they put absolutely no pressure on you to join. Anyone who simply wants a better life is welcome at their meetings. I found them great 'Friends'.